Escaping Apartheid

A Letter to My Mother

NOMANONO ISAACS

Copyright © 2013 by Nomanono Isaacs
GOGO House Publishing

Published by (Publisher of record) House of Penguin Press
www.glcpress.com
All rights reserved by the author.

10 9 8 7 6 5 4 3 2 1   FIRST EDITION

LIBRARY OF CONGRESS CATALOGING-IN-PUBLICATION DATA
Isaacs, Nomanono. 1947—
Escaping Apartheid: A Letter to My Mother / Nomanono Isaacs
p.   cm.

ISBN-13: 978-1482697469   ISBN: 1482697467
1. Life in Apartheid South Africa—Non Fiction. 2. Autobiography / Memoir—
Non Fiction. 3. Political Drama—Non Fiction.   4. British Authors
I. Title

Printed in the United States of America
Set in Palatino Linotype
Book Designed by Lee McCain
Cover Designed by Joachim Alexander
Author Photo by Amy Newstead

Without limiting the rights under copyright reserved above, no part of this publication may be reproduced, stored in or introduced into a retrieval system, or transmitted, in any form or by any means (electronic, mechanical, photocopying, recording, or otherwise), without the prior written permission of both the copyright owner and the above publisher of this book.

The scanning, uploading, and distribution of this book via the Internet or via any other means without the permission of the publisher is illegal and punishable by law. Please purchase only authorised electronic editions, and do not participate in or encourage piracy of copyrightable materials.
Your support of the author's rights is greatly appreciated.

TABLE OF CONTENTS

1. Love, Under a Willow Tree
11

2. Country-less
21

3. Pleasant memories
25

4. The Beginning of the End
43

5. When You Left
65

6. Your Brief Return
73

7. New Job, New Beginning
77

8. Running Away from South Africa
83

9. Tata and Thami
97

10. An Evening with Special Branch
109

11. Road Trip
133

12. The Last Miles
159

13. Epilogue
181

River — with Love

We are all the beautiful colours of the rainbow!

Lots of Love

Nomanono

In loving memory of Malamlela Michael and Nongilandi Gretta Malunga (My parents);

Nkwekhwezi Isaac and MaNovazi Kate Zozo (My maternal grandparents).

Grandpa: Nkwekhwezi means 'Star' and You were and You will always be my Star!

Acknowledgements:

Mandisa Phumla Dumezweni — thank you for your continuing support, guidance, counsel, for your Mama, from the beginning of this project, in various many ways and I cannot thank you enough! And to "Baby" Noma Dumezweni, a Big Thank You for being a sounding board for your Mama!

To my Beautiful friends: Allison Edwards, Vivian Yates, Anne Muddiman, Eliza Lochan, Debbie Diva Bivens — thank you all for your wonderful invaluable support and encouragement.

To the Creative Work Shoppe, the lovely people who edited, designed, and saw this book through to completion — Lee McCain, Joachim Alexander, and Beth McCain — a very hearty thanks. And finally, to Jim Mills: Thank you for being My Proof Reader of Magnitude!

Thank you all from the bottom of my heart.

ESCAPING APARTHEID

A Letter to My Mother

1. LOVE, UNDER A WILLOW TREE

Mama, the year is 1992 and the month is May. We are thousands of miles apart. You are in South Africa and I am in England. It was twenty-four years last Christmas since I saw you. Do you remember the Christmas of 1967? I remember it as though it was yesterday! It was the last time we spent together. There are so many things that I always wished I could tell you about. I always hoped we would meet soon. But soon has turned into many years. Nevertheless I still pray to whoever is out there in the universe that one day we will meet. I pray our old prayers too—to our ancestors.

One evening four years ago I scribbled these lines:

*So many times I have told myself
Life has to go on anyway.
For there is so much I want to do.
I have told myself
Life is short and has to be lived,
In my case, through hard work;
Feeling homesick is not going to help me.
So I convince myself.
But every second of my waking day
I have a constant heartbeat – VERY
    PAINFUL!*

*Sometimes I have detached myself successfully
From the feeling that somewhere, something
Very important in my life is missing.
The family I left behind.*

*You see, I used to cry a lot.
Nowadays I tell myself
I am tough, strong and life has to go on.
But I am haunted by the images I hold in
    my mind*

ESCAPING APARTHEID
A Letter To My Mother

Of my twelve- and nine-year-old brothers.
They were that age—when I last saw them.
They are old men today.

As for my mother,
She was 42 years old when I last saw her.
Today she is 64.
But images still, are those
Of a beautiful 42-year-old.

I tell myself, I'm tough and strong.
I must carry on regardless.
But suddenly, it hits me.
I can't hold my tears any more.
I let them flow down my cheeks
When I am on my own—no one about.
With the wrenching pain between my
 breasts

Yes, I am homesick.

I am forty-four now and two years older than the age you were when we were last together. Right now, I imagine you at the age of forty-two, the age you were on our last Christmas together in 1967. You were very beautiful, very fair without a blemish on your face, except a very tiny red mole the size of a pinhead, close to the corner of your eye. You won't believe this, but it pains me so much at this moment, the fact that I can't remember on which eye it was. You had such lovely legs and I always wished that I could have had legs like yours. But I was always told that mine resembled those of my paternal grandfather Samuel, as did all my features.

Over the years I have had a chance to reflect and evaluate everything about our life together up to the time I left. I feel you should know what I felt and what it was like, since we never really had a chance to talk. I have no intention of hurting your feelings. It was not your fault that I had to leave. There are so many things you had no control over and you hurt at the time and we hurt with you.

You had no control over all the hardships that faced us during the Christmas of 1967. At the time you were working as a domestic servant in a white residential area in Pietermaritzburg. You worked for Etienne's parents. I never knew their surname except that they were British. I had just completed

ESCAPING APARTHEID
A Letter To My Mother

my final examinations at Sigcawu Teacher Training College and had come home for Christmas.

At that time you were living at Mabulala, one of Machibisa's slums. Mabulala was crowded with badly built mud huts, shanties and shacks made out of anything that people could get hold of. Ours was a mixture of mud, rusty corrugated iron sheeting and cardboards. The roof was made of that rusty corrugated iron sheeting, while the walls were of mud held by twigs that were coiled round the poles dug deep into the ground.

The windows were of planks while cardboards, supported by corrugated iron sheeting, formed partitions that created rooms in our mud hut. You still paid rent to an Indian landlady who lived in an old big concrete house with a roof of old rusty corrugated iron sheeting that looked as though it had seen better days. And its faded red paint revealed huge, cracked patches that always gave an impression that the whole roof would collapse any time.

Your Indian landlady's house had a large veranda where she sat frying bajis on a paraffin primus stove. She was always shouting at her little boys of about nine and eleven, ordering them to go fetch things and also to take the bajis to the tuck shop that she owned, which had very few things for sale.

You know, I did not like the bajis from that tuck shop because it was not clean. Her boys were never in clean clothes either. I can still remember the smell of fried chilli-peppered bajis.

There were many mud huts in her yard belonging to different tenants. To get to ours we had to go past a stinking pit lavatory that was used by all the tenants. The stench was unbearable at times when you had run out of jeyes fluid, which we carried to the lavatory during times when we had no alternative but to use it. In most cases we avoided using it.

I visited you at work so that I could use the servants' toilets instead. There were no rubbish bins in the yard so there was this pile of garbage in one corner. It stunk of rotting cabbage and onions. People just threw everything there including the urine that had been kept in chamber pots or old billy cans during the night. Very early in the morning some people would just throw the urine in the garbage tip instead of the pit toilet.

In the summer, when it was hot, the blue bottle flies used to have a feast on that garbage tip. The smells sometimes were a shitty methane gas type and at other times they were a pungent and corrosive odour.

I always resented the setup in Pietermaritzburg. It seemed so unfair that there should be such a huge slum with people living in squalor, so close to such a very rich town. At that time I did not know any other big town or city in South Africa other than Pietermaritzburg. It was a town that was very busy with many wealthy white and Indian people. Well, to me they looked wealthy!

Walking along Long Market Street with a huge buzz of city life, busy traffic and crowds of people in the streets and roads, for me as a village girl, was frightening at first. I used to wonder sometimes how people knew where they were going. If you remember, I also asked the same question of you, wondering how come you never got lost, as I was even afraid to get into buses on my own to your place of work. I had no trouble getting into trains from

Kokstad because it was a very small town. But travelling from Pietermaritzburg train station to the surrounding locations was a huge scary thing for me. But later I got it.

The other thing that I resented so much, which I believe was at the root of all my miseries, was the fact that you had been forced to leave the village where we had lived because of rehabilitation schemes (even now I still resent that) but I will tell you later how I really felt about them.

Well, during that Christmas you had no money. You were paid R8.00 (eight rands) a month. Do you remember? Please then don't blame yourself for the fact that on that Christmas day we sat under a willow tree outside our shanty in Mabulala and drank water. I know that even though my kid brothers were twelve and nine, they understood the situation very much, just like I did. In fact we all felt for you. We felt the pain you were going through.

You were feeling guilty and felt a failure because you had not been able to provide a proper Christmas meal for us. If you remember, it was Monwabisi, who was twelve,

ESCAPING APARTHEID
A Letter To My Mother

who came up with a brilliant idea that cheered us up. Upon his clever suggestion we all got out and swept the yard in front of our shack early that morning so as to appear busy getting ready for the big festivities and I have never forgotten what he said.

He said, since everyone around us kept their places filthy, we would seem better off because we were a clean and tidy family and no one would really notice that we did not have food. We did exactly that and in fact forgot that we did not have anything to celebrate Christmas with. Instead we went out and sat under the willow tree, with you mending someone's suit with your Singer sewing machine. Do you still have that sewing machine?

I will always remember the love we shared. You gave so much under that willow tree. It was the four of us. You, Monwabisi, Khayalethu, and I—just turned twenty then. The fact that we were caught in such poverty on that particular day taught me a lot and I often think of it. Had we had food and all that goes with Christmas festivities, I would not have realised just how much love existed in all four of us. You were there for us. What we had was special that day. You kept saying had you had two cents for the bus fare you would have gone to help Etienne's mother during the morning so that you could bring to us her Christmas leftovers.

At first we tried looking everywhere for cents. We turned pockets inside out and checked every possible place that might by chance had a cent. But had you gone to work, it would have been obvious to the neighbours that something was amiss. But because you were there, telling us stories and jokes, we had so much laughter and were very happy. We even forgot that there was no food and we had the best Christmas in the midst of poverty.

2. COUNTRY-LESS

What you did not know was the resentment I had towards the system that had made us semi-human beings. I did not like seeing your life an endless struggle for survival. I felt that the whole situation had been imposed on so many of us. I was angry and resentful all the time. I saw happiness being taken away by force from us and the nights you spent knitting, crocheting or sewing made me hate South Africa. At that time, I confess, I hated everybody who was white.

Do you remember the day two white boys, aged between nine and ten, set an Alsatian dog on you as you walked past their house on your way home from work? Do you remember that

Etienne's mother with her British ways thought she would fight for you because the whole thing was appalling, and she assumed she would file a complaint on your behalf, but she never succeeded? I know it was noble of her to try and help her black employee. But that was South Africa.

When you told me about the boys and the Alsatian dog, I cried because I was angry, frustrated and above all, helpless. When you said they started laughing as you were screaming for help and they shouted 'kaffir' several times, I felt that being black in South Africa was worse than being in hell. What's more, the dogs had a better place and were treated better than us blacks. As blacks, our status was below that of a dog!

After the dog incident, I could not trust anyone and I hated the South African Apartheid system with all my soul. I felt I did not belong in South Africa, the country I was born in. I felt I was country-less. I was nobody in my own country because of the colour of my skin. Oh, I hated that with every fibre of my being! I hated a situation where I could not question why certain things that were happening were so unjust.

For instance, do you remember when you worked at Hutchinson Road? You could live in the servants' quarters but you could not let Tata (father) visit you openly. There were frequent raids during the nights from the police and whenever Tata visited you, you had to do your best to hide him. I was allowed to stay with you because I was a girl. Now, what sort of life was that, in a country where your own husband had to creep in to visit you?

All this had to be accepted by all women who worked in white residential areas. To me it was just another law that made me angrier and hate even more. You had to ask for permission from your white employer each time I was about to visit you. All this, I knew, was making you feel helpless and sad.

3. PLEASANT MEMORIES

Let me tell you about the good things. Firstly, having been outside South Africa for twenty-five years at this point, and having travelled to other countries and lived with people of different races, nationalities and different colours, I can today say that I am glad I was born in South Africa. And I am glad I had you as my mother.

South Africa is a country that breeds hatred against and amongst races. The Apartheid system is damaging and poisonous because it creates fears and distrust amongst its nationals. The huge hatred the system of South Africa has created is based on peoples' colours. It is a divide and rule system that is very cruel. People are graded on colour and the texture of their hair.

Over the years I have become strong in spirit and I do not hate anymore. I am aware that I don't have to like a person because of the colour of their skin. I don't have to like a white person nor do I have to like a black person. I like a person just because of what and who they are.

If you asked me whether I remember the village I grew up in, I would tell you this: I was born in the village of Makhanya. This is in Umzimkhulu District. Umzimkhulu district is named after Umzimkhulu River which forms part of the border between Natal and the Cape Province.

Makhanya is part of Nyaka area, Nyaka being a huge forest on a mountain overlooking the village. To the east of Makhanya is another village set below and behind a mountain, called Gudlintaba. I remember that both villages were surrounded by various hills and mountains. We used to walk in the hills and mountains while looking after the grazing cattle. At first, Makhanya had few inhabitants and before the rehabilitation schemes it was a close knit community.

Everyone was helpful and would rally round whenever there was someone in need. It was the same on the other side of the mountain too, at Gudlintaba, where Grandpa Isaac and Grandma Kate lived.

Some other good memories I have about our life together are Saturdays in autumn when we joined other villagers to go to Nyaka forest to collect firewood in preparation for the cold winter nights and days. Those outings were 'working picnics'. We took food and drinks with us as we were out all day. We walked distances of two to three miles. We would sing on the way.

I remember I used to sing at the top of my voice because I was told I had a very strong voice. You had a beautiful sweet soprano voice: remember the songs you used to teach us and how patient you were with me when I could not pick up tunes easily?

Just before we reached Nyaka forest, we would pass Nyaka Primary School and the stream that we used every Friday after cleaning the classrooms. It was a stream that was used to clean up all the buckets and basins that we had used for carrying cow dung to smear on the mud floors as this was a very good way of preserving the floors.

I was about ten or eleven years old when we had these forest trips. All the grown-ups helped us with our bundles of wood. They prepared them in such a way that prevented them from either sagging or breaking into two as we carried them on our heads on the way home. Two to three miles on foot at the time seemed a long distance to me, especially on the way home when the older women would put us through a fast pace while carrying our bundles. But what I remember is the happiness, laughter, a spirit of well-being and kinship in a small village.

Deep in the forest I felt so small, and yet so free! For me, the forest represented a feeling of awe and I felt part of it and I was grateful to be able to freely dig edible roots, with your guidance. The wild sour berries we used to pick! You taught me to climb trees, to break dry twigs or branches. I know you all made us aware that collecting fire wood was not in any way intended to destroy the forest. Nobody destroyed it. It was forbidden to chop healthy trees but our purpose was just to clear and pick those that had died naturally. There was something very special about that particular forest, something I felt: forest noises, our voices echoing. I liked the echoes best! What I felt was freedom of my whole being! When deep in the forest, looking up through the spaces between branches of very tall trees, seeing the blue sky.

I can still remember the musty smells of rotting leaves and bark. The thick thorny dense parts that we avoided and the tiny foot tracks that were evidence of regular visitations from firewood collectors. I remember the picnic areas that we used and the streams that we used for drinking water when deep in the forest.

You did a lot of good things for us. I recall you helping with my multiplication tables when I started schooling. You taught me to count and write long before I went to school. I remember the first day there when Miss Ngcobo taught us the alphabet. I was the clever one because I could recognise all the letters of the alphabet while they were new to the other children.

I could count up to one hundred long before I started school. You had encouraged me using my sisters' books and from the knowledge you gained when you were an assistant Primary School teacher at St George's Primary, just across Cabane River on a low-lying field towards Ngqokozweni village. You did this work before you got married. You took pleasure in teaching all three of us. That was before my brothers were born. For that, thank you. You taught us a lot by good examples. You were never rude to anybody. You respected your elders and we too learnt to respect elders.

You also changed Grandpa Isaac's attitude towards educating girls. Had you not fled at the age of fourteen in search of a higher primary school, and went to Ntsikeni which is over a hundred miles to the north of Makhanya village, Grandpa would have continued paying for boys to be educated and thereby discriminating against the girls—as it was the norm with most people of his generation.

ESCAPING APARTHEID
A Letter To My Mother

They assumed that a girl's place was in marrying and settling down, to having children as soon as she reached puberty. Today there are many women in those two villages who were able to have education at that time just because you were brave.

You travelled at night through ready-to-harvest maize fields, and crossed Cabane River. You went through Myembe village and Myembe hills and mountains, looking for a place you had never been to. You slept rough for two nights and travelled during the day but through kind people who gave you food and 'amarhewu' (sour drink made from maize porridge and very nice when mixed with sugar) on the way, you never starved when you had run out of the food you had taken from home for your journey.

But luck and your ancestors were guiding you all the way because on the third day you were helped by people who knew the family you wanted to go to. They were on horseback which in those days was the only easy way to travel long distances. They gave you a ride to Ntsikeni. As you were an established horse rider, you proved an easy companion to the kind strangers. Even though you had never met your relatives but only heard that they lived close to the higher primary school you wanted to be educated in, you had made a very brave decision indeed.

But I only mention this marvellous act in passing. What I suppose I want to tell you is that I valued and treasured the life we had in the village up to the time I was eleven years old. It is just that up to that age I felt at home and I felt I belonged somewhere. I also remember the village shop that was about twelve miles away from home. It was called Cabane Store. Going to Cabane Store was a highlight of many Saturdays.

That shop stocked everything. It was a truly "general store" for the many surrounding villages. It sold cheap cosmetics, coats and jackets for men, all types of fabrics for women and children. It sold sugar, tea, soap, lard and tobacco, just to mention a few. The shop owner was a white man and there was no other shop in the area. His shop served neighbouring villages of about twenty to thirty miles away.

ESCAPING APARTHEID
A Letter To My Mother

I used to take the trips to Cabane Store as outings. We used to go in groups with friends on many occasions but I would go on my own when there were items that were urgently required. On those days, I would run most of the way and I would be back home in no time at all and you would shower me with praises, which I enjoyed a lot.

With friends, we sang songs, trying hard to teach ourselves many of the new and popular songs of that time. The funny thing about our songs was that we never bothered to find out the meaning of the songs so long as they were popular new English songs. Those who had gramophones in their homes and listened to English songs would come up with words or phrases that sounded nearer to what they heard. We would then end up with songs that had different meanings from their original compositions as we did not understand English that much, either. But we did not care, for we were happy and enjoyed ourselves.

The singing made our travelling a lot easier as we went up the hills and down the slopes, finding our way carefully down some rocky and frightful dongas (huge crevices on the ground caused by soil erosion). We looked forward to buying some penny or farthing sweets (before currency changed to Rand and Cent). Penny-worth of sweets were our reward from whoever had sent us on a shopping errand. Most villagers bought from the shop what they called 'white man's stuff' — meaning sugar, tea, white bread and white buns. It was a novelty to buy white bread as most people baked their own rough brown bread from millet flour. White sugar was also used or taken as something special. Most villagers thought it was more interesting than the cheap brown sugar they so frequently used.

What I found most interesting on these shopping trips was feasting on the black lumps of brown sugar that we often found amongst the sacks of brown sugar. We mixed these lumps with water and made a very thick dark brown sweet drink and dunked chunks of white bread or buns in. We used to stop for a break by a stream and feast on this and various other things that people bought. I really enjoyed stuffing myself; you do remember, don't you?

ESCAPING APARTHEID
A Letter To My Mother

Another pleasant memory is of the day Tata (father) came to meet me one freezing winter day on my way from school. It had been a very cold winter day and the teachers had decided to let us go home early. But I had been very cold. Other children started running and I could not keep up with them. As you know, all of us children in the village went to school bare feet, even on cold winter days. My feet were frozen and I felt very stiff.

Because you had seen other children go past our house without me, Tata had decided to come and meet me. He was on leave from work, and when I saw him I got very excited and very happy. I felt very loved and taken care of. But the truth was, I could have run with the other children but because I wanted to see if Tata would come and take care of me, I stayed behind pretending that I could not run anymore. And it worked! Tata proved his love and care to me. But you both knew because he teased me afterwards and we all laughed about it.

That day, Tata promised to save money to buy us shoes for the following winter. And true to his word, when he visited on his following annual leave, he brought me a beautiful red coat while my sister, Nosipho, had a pink one. They were of the same style, just different colours. They were beautiful coats.

He also bought us very beautiful black leather shoes. I became known in the village as 'little red coat' and I did not mind the nickname because I was very proud of my beautiful red coat. It took us a while to get used to wearing shoes. At first it felt awkward and the shoes pinched our toes. We stuffed the shoes with wet paper until they softened, allowing us to wear them comfortably. That was the year before everything changed.

My life up to the age of eleven years was nothing but a contented village life. I had everything. By this I mean warmth, love, security and above all, a sense of belonging. I belonged to a very close-knit community as well as a very loving extended family. There was Grandpa Isaac and grandma Kate, your parents, on the other side of the mountain at Gudlintaba, providing love and security for all of us.

ESCAPING APARTHEID
A Letter To My Mother

At Makhanya there was the Malunga family (father's) providing the same. At that age we always knew that we would have someone to turn to in times of difficulties. If you remember, I was very close to father, but closer to both Grandpa Isaac and Grandma Kate, your parents.

Even though we lived at Makhanya village, we seemed to be living at Gudlintaba just the same. This was due to the love of Grandpa and Grandma. Every school holiday I spent with them. I had lived with them up to the time just before I had to start school. But this did not stop us going over the mountain every weekend. You loved going back to your parents just like we did. There were times I would come home from school to find Grandpa talking to you and you were both so happy in each other's company. He loved you very much. Grandma Kate loved me very much and I loved her. I loved both of them.

The strange thing is I still miss them even today. They died twenty-nine years ago today and yes, I do miss them. We had such freedom and felt so protected by them. They worked hard for all the wealth they had. We enjoyed the fruits of their labour, literally. Grandpa would bring us fruit from his orchard or maize and vegetables from his fields. The times I liked most were when he brought us his home made 'Amasi' (sour milk).

You remember that huge orchard? He had oranges, apricots, figs, plums, lemons, peaches. The fruit I liked most were peaches, apricots and figs. Do you remember the respect that everyone gave your parents? They earned their respect by being kind, generous, good listeners and understanding. Grandpa's home was open to everyone amongst the Gudlintaba villagers. He helped those who were in need. Not only did people come for material help, but for advice on personal matters. Grandpa was a community and family leader.

I used to enjoy helping Grandpa, especially during the hoeing period. There would be family members as well as people from the village who came to hoe. Grandpa's duty was to help make hoeing easier for everyone by using two oxen that pulled a weeder which he held with both his hands and moved between the rows of crops.

The weeder was heavy equipment that needed skill and Grandpa was the best at it. My job was to lead the two oxen between the rows of crops. There was a leather rope that was tied to the yoke that the oxen were harnessed onto. It was quite long as to avoid the big oxen trampling on me or poking me with their horns.

They were beautiful oxen. One of them was a bit dangerous with its horns. They were called Vryman and Van Uys. Van Uys was the dangerous one. He could at an instant charge with his horn at anyone who annoyed him. On this particular day, I am sure you remember because you were amongst the women and young girls who were hoeing up on the field.

I did not want to help Grandpa. I felt that I was going to miss a lot of fun with my cousins joining in the singing that was going on and I would be pulling the oxen guiding them along. I had asked grandpa if I could do just half the area that we were working on and let someone else to come and swap with me. Grandpa had refused, saying that I was the best at that job and he needed me. I sulked and thought, "Well, I am not really going to help Grandpa today. I will walk slowly so that he never finishes what he wants to do anyway."

As I walked in front of the oxen, Grandpa kept yelling at Van Uys and Vryman, thinking that they were not pulling as they should. He used his whip that he always carried while holding on to the weeder. When he whipped them, they moved a bit faster so I gathered my pace.

But as we continued, everything seemingly going fine, I started thinking about the fun I was missing and I thought I am going to go slow again. I had become very lazy as well because it was hot; I felt sleepy. I could not ask grandpa for a break because it was not yet time for a break. I just started thinking different things forgetting my job.

The next thing you will remember I was screaming at the top of my voice straddled at the back of Van Uys! He had just scooped me from the back between my legs with his horn and threw me on his back. Did I scream! All the singing that was going on from all of you women and girls who were hoeing came to a sudden stop! The whole valley must have heard me. Grandpa was so fast and I do not know how he did it at the time, but he caught me and safely put me down. He comforted me and told me that it was time I had a break for the whole afternoon!

Later, though, Grandpa teased me saying that he had watched me walking lazily and knew that Van Uys was going to get me out of his way. Grandpa said he also wanted to teach me a lesson that no one sleeps or forgets what their job is while they are engaged in it. He said Van Uys was temperamental but not really harmful. Grandpa knew that all he was going to do was scoop me as I was a lot shorter than him and he had long horns. So when he did, Grandpa was ready. Grandpa said he had seen it before with Van Uys. From that day I never fell asleep in front of two oxen. I was alert and diligent. It was the only time and the last that I was ever angry with Grandpa.

4. THE BEGINNING OF THE END

But do you remember the sudden change that happened in 1959? Well, I'll take you back. It was like this, or rather this is the way I experienced it: At first rumours spread around the community that our villages were going to be either moved completely or changed, and the term that was used was rehabilitation.

Some people were against the scheme and others did not know what to make of it. I came home and asked you if you had heard what I had been told by some children at school; that our village was going to be moved. At that stage you said you had also heard varying rumours and you told me not to worry about what I heard, for no matter what happened, we'd be together.

Those words were comforting. I proudly told you that whatever the government wanted to do to our villages, Grandpa Isaac would definitely see to it that we remained where we were. You smiled and did not say a word but told me to get changed from my khaki dress which was my school uniform.

You see, Grandpa Isaac was such a tower of strength to me and because everyone in the village respected him, in my young innocent mind, at that age, I was definitely sure that he would advise all those who wanted to rehabilitate the villages to change their minds.

The rumours persisted and they were different and contradictory every day. There was unspoken and unexpressed fear. Some children heard parents talking in harsh and grave tones about the future that seemed very bleak indeed. Our lives were going to be changed.

The children who came from families close to the community sibondas (governors) knew more but there were also rumours that villagers were being split by arguments that were going on. There were those who did not want to abide by the laws that were soon going to be introduced and wanted to fight the wicked white men (as they put it) to the last man. They said if it meant death it did not matter for they would be fighting for their forefathers' land and their own rights to remain in those lands without interference from the whites.

There were also those who thought it was futile trying to fight or resist the white government of South Africa as it would do whatever it wanted anyway without listening to the views of a race that it saw as inferior. Even so, those opposed to the scheme felt that they had a right to their land and the villages in which they had lived for generations. They did not see what right a white person, in some government office, had of deciding on other peoples' future just because they were black.

This began mistrust amongst the villagers. People became suspicious of one another because those who did not know which way to decide were suspected of working with the government, so were those who thought it was pointless fighting. Did you know that I felt very confused about all this?

I also remember feeling very scared of the unknown. There were children at school who really believed that rehabilitation schemes would be good. They had half heard their aunts and uncles saying the villages would be turned into places like KwaMashu in Durban or Machibisa in Pietermaritzburg. Since most children in our school had never been to Durban nor Pietermaritzburg, we then imagined beautiful things happening and the government turning the villages into fantastic places. We pictured our village being like Durban or even Johannesburg for that matter, having street lights, electricity for all our domestic chores, just like it was in the cities, so we thought!

There was so much confusion and excitement. Others came back with views that their parents had expressed of situations that would lead to crime. I understood little at the time. At the back of my mind I thought if we were to live like those people who lived in the townships in Durban and Johannesburg, we would certainly be going places. I imagined myself going to school wearing shoes instead of walking bare feet. I had no clue what life was like in the townships of South Africa. We all thought that the people in those townships led a better life than us in the villages.

I even told you that the new change meant that we were all going to have sophisticated things such as the opportunity to learn to use knives and forks properly because civilised and sophisticated people used them. You laughed when I said this, saying that using knives and forks had nothing to do with sophistication as it was a cultural thing.

At that time I did not understand very much. I was also excited about the possibility of having indoor lavatories. Our imaginations at school had gone wild! We laughed a lot as we listed things that might be of good change with the rehabilitation schemes. We thought we would not need to carry buckets on our heads from the local wells as we would have water taps indoors just like in the stories I had heard from my elder sister, telling us about life in her college (at Lourdes Roman Catholic Boarding College) that they did not have to go outside for water.

Do you remember the afternoon I came running home, so excited? All the excitement was bubbling in me, after the marvellous day we had had at school speculating about what exciting new life we were going to have in the village. I told you as soon as I stepped in, hardly waiting to change from my school clothes. I was filled with the excitement of the future in our new village, as imagined by us school children. I didn't even see someone sitting on a stool behind the door that was left open to let the afternoon breeze in. The funny thing was that I had even forgotten about the other rumours that the villagers were split and were ready to fight one another. You listened earnestly until I paused. You smiled, turned and looked towards the door. It was Grandpa Isaac you were looking at! He had a sad smile on his face. I rushed over with my arms wide open to hug him and sat on his lap as was always the case when he visited us.

He kissed me on my cheek and hugged me without saying a word. He listened while I enthusiastically continued about the new life, saying that he wouldn't have to ride his horse, Qhali, when travelling. Instead there would be buses—like they had in Durban and Johannesburg—as I was told. There might even be the trams I had learnt about at school. I did not see any reason why we would not have them, since we were going to have electricity and everything that was civilised. You both listened to me as if what I was saying was very interesting.

Yes, at the time it was interesting as far as I was concerned. But for both of you it was interesting for very different reasons.

You both listened without sharing in my enthusiasm. I suppose you listened because you never interrupted people, as you both believed that we all deserved to be listened to. I suppose too that it was your patience! I was never patient, you know that. I am still fighting a tendency to interrupt when people talk. Even though I know it is rude to interrupt, my impatience tends to get the better of me.

I am working at this and I hope one of these days I will succeed in being patient and be more like you and Grandpa. If I were to be honest with you, I could never understand your patience when I was young. I always wanted things to happen like yesterday. But I am really working at it and I am learning that things happen when it is the right time for them to happen!

But Grandpa's uneasy move alerted me to stop talking. I sensed that something was wrong. In fact I realised for the first time since entering the rondavel that Grandpa was very much different from his usual self.

I stood up, saying I was going to take off my school clothes and put on my casual wear. The truth is I suddenly felt very scared. I knew something was terribly wrong because I had never seen Grandpa so unhappy before. He looked like someone who had lost someone very special. I immediately got worried about Grandma. Somehow, I did not want to hear whatever was troubling Grandpa. You also looked very sad. I just felt cold and wanted to put things right. Whatever was troubling the two of you, I wished it could just go away and I did not even wish to know what it was.

I then realised that you had been crying before I returned from school. I wanted to scream but did not know what for. I felt pain at whatever was paining you both. I started imagining the worst. Perhaps Grandma Kate was dead or was it uncle Israel? Was it Tata? If it was Tata I would have known earlier at school as there would have been someone to bring me home and you would have been surrounded by other villagers and elderly women. So Tata was alive. If it was Grandma, Grandpa would not be here of course. He would have been at Gudlintaba sitting in silence with the corpse and also with very close relatives, all elderly. So that sorted Grandma. I was pleased she was alive. It was likely to be uncle, your brother. But again, there would have been someone else who came to tell us, not Grandpa. These thoughts went like a flash through my mind as I was changing my clothes.

    I came back to where you both were after changing. I felt awkward, not knowing how to behave after all my earlier excitement. But thankfully Grandpa soon put me straight. He told me that all that we imagined with my school friends as glorious was not at all going to be so. There was going to be suffering instead, he said. He told me that we lived a far richer life in values of humanity and self sufficiency in the villages than those people who grew up in townships. Our lives had been, up to that point, based on real family units, he said.

He said that for us village children, life in a township was bound to appear exciting and far better than that of our village. There was hardship in townships. People did not have land to grow what they wanted. They did not have land to graze and breed live stock like he and other villagers had. Without money, it was difficult to survive in the townships and because of that, people turned to crime as means of survival. He said he did not wish that sort of life on any of his family, especially when there were so many of us who would need a decent education.

As you know, Grandpa provided school fees for all my older cousins and everyone expected him to. He also took the education side of the family as his task. Was it because you made him feel guilty by running away in search of education as a girl? At any rate, Grandpa was a pillar of strength and inspiration for all the family.

Grandpa was in pain trying to make me understand. He was the one who explained everything to me. He told me that in those villages everyone had been self sufficient without the use of electricity. He pointed to his wealth and rightly said that up to then he had never needed electricity. The natural light that God had provided had been enough for everyone and he felt this would continue to be so for a long time.

At that point he asked me if I wanted to know how he had accumulated so much wealth. I said yes, then he looked at his Zobo watch which he kept in his jacket pocket, attached with a beautiful silver chain, then shook his head saying perhaps next time. It was the time he went, for the sun would be setting soon and he needed to round up the cattle, goats, sheep and horses on his way home in order to lock them up for the night.

But before he went he said, "I will just tell you this: the white government of South Africa has decided that we are not worth being treated as humans. Another thing, I know; very few people in the whole family know how many cattle I possess. No one knows how many horses I own. You don't know how many apricot, peach, orange, plum, lemon and fig trees I have." Just then I interrupted, feeling clever. It was a mistake I should not have made. I said, "You have three fig trees." It was the look on his eyes that was a mixture of anger and disgust, for he really did not need anyone's answers, that is, literally.

To him it was a way of expressing his burning anger, hurt, and helplessness that he was going through. It is true most of us did not know how many cattle, sheep, goats and horses he had... well, with the exception of the three fig trees which everyone knew—not just me, the clever one of course! But he knew each and every one of his animals in his land. He had never been to school but had taught himself to count. He knew each and every animal just like he knew all of us in his extended family. The animals were his family and he did not take them for granted like most of us young people.

Grandpa had worked from absolutely nothing to achieve what he had. His final words were, "I have to destroy or get rid of some of them, and have only what I am told by this white government. I have had enough in this world and have experienced so much hardship but I never thought that I would experience anything like this.

"You are all going to be very poor," he said, "and the whole family will experience hardship. My heart goes out to you, Nomanono and your sisters and brothers, because I will never be able to pay for your school fees like I paid for your cousins. This is what brought me here today to tell your mother the bad news."

Grandpa went on to tell me that there were many families who were going to break up. A lot of people would have to go to the cities to find employment to support themselves or their families. The farming that the villagers had depended on was going to be a thing of the past. It was not just live stock that was required to be reduced, but land also had to be reduced.

As if that was not enough, everyone had to move homes. It was an order. Nobody had a choice. The whole thing was callous. At his old age he was expected to start from scratch to build a home on a plot of land that he did not even choose. His several acres of land had to go. He had always wanted to be buried close to the graves of his parents, but now he had no clue where his grave would be.

As Grandpa continued, you had tears in your eyes. I cried. You did not cry because I was there with you. You wanted to be strong for me. What hurt me most was when he said, "We are treated as though we belong to another country but not South Africa. It is the white man's colour-bar. I have lived in this land all of my life and I have helped a lot of people realise their hopes and ambitions in whatever small way, in this village," he said.

"We have all worked together and a lot of other villagers have helped me too. Right now I feel helpless. The whole thing is humiliating for me. To have to come here and tell my own daughter and grandchild that they are going to be paupers not before long is very painful and very hard for me."

I realised then what hard a task Grandpa had. We expected so much from him. He also felt that he had to fulfil everyone's needs and yet he could not anymore. The truth was, even so, I still hoped that with his wisdom he would come out with the right solution. I was only eleven years old. I had lived a very comfortable and protected life with all of you around me. Grandpa felt that he was letting everyone down. He felt guilty but he should not have done because it was something beyond his control.

The other thing I wanted to tell you about was that once I found him by the cattle kraal sobbing. I had never in my entire life seen Grandpa cry. Seeing him crying so helplessly began the hatred I told you about earlier. To me he had always been a tower of strength and I could not imagine him breaking down. Moreover, in the society I was brought up, men do not cry only wimps do. The only accepted circumstances for any man to cry were death.

But as he sobbed, he now and again uttered a few words. I stood there frozen and listened to what he was saying. What was biting deep into his heart was the feeling of helplessness. I loved him very much and I still do. I did not think him a wimp for crying. I understood clearly he could not help anybody, let alone himself. He did not want to part with his animals. He called the names of those which were his favourites but he loved all the animals as we all know. He had to keep a certain number and sell the rest but there was not going to be much money for those he sold. So it was all a waste of many years of toil, gone down the drain.

Everyone was to keep a few that would be needed for a span of oxen to use in the fields. What those in power did not care to think was that it was not right to keep using the same oxen for ploughing because they needed rest. It was therefore important to have a variety to choose from and that helped keep the cattle healthy, fit and strong.

So you see, the white government of South Africa and those who supported it, indirectly or directly, shattered our lives. It was very hard for me, as an eleven-year-old, to see and feel the pain that so many people where going through. For me it was as if the pain was beyond everyone else's for I felt mostly for Grandpa, you and the whole family. The fantasies that we had at school had now vanished. Everyone had come to realise that there were no indoor toilets to come and people would still continue to carry buckets of water on their heads. They would only be allowed to get the water in designated areas.

In most cases the streams and wells that people had been using were now in the areas that were dedicated to grazing only. New wells had to be found in new settlements.

The village was covered with a feeling of foreboding. Not many people smiled and sung songs happily anymore. Those who resisted change and did not want to move had their homes bulldozed. This was the worst situation and it was very painful to watch people who had nothing to begin with, having the little that they had, pulled down and flattened by government bulldozers. Most of those affected lived on the mountains alongside Nyaka forest. The pain that people felt was deep and mixed with both anger and hate.

For us as a family too it was hard, just as Grandpa had predicted. Our huts had to be built a few yards from where they were originally and this meant that the existing ones had to be demolished to abide by the regulations. Tata's job did not pay enough money for all that was now required. Without Grandpa's cattle, there were not enough oxen to help us plough the fields, which had been allocated on a very barren area. The whole set-up stunk and it was very painful. That was the beginning of the end for us in the village of Makhanya because you had to uproot yourself and go find a job to help us through.

You became very withdrawn. But you still continued to sing lullabies and tell us stories whenever you were not very tired at night. The rehabilitation schemes destroyed the security we had as a family. That extended family unit was dismantled. Grandpa lost inner will to fight and live. From that time onwards he became a weak man in health and, above all, in spirit. It was painful to see him lose all his wealth in such a brutal manner. He was not the only wealthy man who experienced the pain. The villages were never the same after that. The closeness that we had had disappeared. Most people in the village had to go to the cities to find jobs.

Jobs in the cities did not come easy. Even when they found jobs, finding accommodation was difficult and costly. The reality of the rehabilitation schemes was soon clear to all members of the village community we once had. It was harsh the way people were stripped of the freedom they were enjoying.

The sense of belonging was gone. From that period, I never felt I belonged to South Africa. I felt I did not belong anywhere. I still don't belong anywhere.

5. WHEN YOU LEFT

What was our crime? Why were we punished? Just because we were not white we had to go through that hell? What right does any human being have to suppress another human being in such a dreadful manner? Who said being white was the most important thing that ever happened in the creation of the universe? What right does the white South Africans have of denying other races that are non-white freedom to live in the same country under the same conditions and rights that they themselves enjoy?

As you know, when you left we went to live at Gudlintaba with Grandpa Isaac and Grandma Kate. It was painful when you left.

Even though I knew that going to live with Grandpa and Grandma was the best thing because I loved them, it was somehow different this time, because you were going to be away for an indefinite period. I had never lived without you for a long time except during the school holidays when I visited my grandparents because to me that was my holiday. Grandma cried when you had just left. We all cried.

It was hardest for Grandpa because he had to be strong for us and he did not want to break. At that time father was very quiet too and we did not know what had happened to him. The letters he used to write had dried up but later we learnt that he had joined the Pan African Congress and had lost his job. Every bad thing seemed to happen just at the same time. But at the time even if he had told us about what he was involved in, I do not think I would have understood. I just wanted my family the way it had been before. But it was not the same anymore.

Grandpa was going through a very hard time emotionally. He worried about you a lot. We waited for letters that came from you. You mentioned in the letters that you did not earn enough money and had found a job as a domestic servant somewhere in Mooi River. Your main problem was finding a place to sleep after work because they did not have servant's quarters where you worked. You did not have enough money to rent any kind of accommodation. That really tore us into pieces.

Grandpa cursed the whites in South Africa. Grandma's pain showed constantly in her sad face. It was never the same after you left. The huge orchard that Grandpa had, had been turned into grazing land, by government order on rehabilitation. He tried the hardest to protect everything but it was all so futile because with the last harvest after the rehabilitation schemes were introduced, he had no right to the orchard. The fruits were sold but a lot went to waste.

With the orchard now being part of the grazing land, the rest of the fruit trees were destroyed by animals. There was bitterness. As if all this was not enough, everyone was later forced to have 'dom pas' (a fool's pass) — a registration card. It was an insult to everyone.

There were long queues, people waiting on hot sunny days, for their photographs to be taken for the ID Cards. But Grandma used to make me laugh sometimes by her comments on people's photos when they showed smiles, by saying, "What on earth possessed them to smile, I just don't see why people are smiling on their photos!" And then she would pull different funny faces with her teeth showing, which was what made me laugh. She would say, "I am not going to have any smile on my face because there is absolutely nothing to smile about. The whole process of standing here waiting for the stupid photographs to be taken is very annoying, ugly and demeaning."

As far as the people in the village were concerned, being declared independent and self governing under the Transkei Homeland (Bantustan) was another way of making sure that blacks did not get anywhere. It did not need an educated person to really understand what was happening. Grandpa and many elders in the village had never been to school but they were brilliant, intelligent peasants who were not easily fooled. They obeyed the orders because they had no choice. They were too old to go on fighting. All they wanted was now to die and be with their ancestors. And even if they had tried to fight the government, they would have been declared Communists, a very 'dirty word' in South Africa during those days, as anyone who expressed an opposing opinion against that of the government was labelled a communist.

Up to 1959 I had never even thought much of the politics of South Africa as I was blissfully happy with my family and had felt protected. But I experienced and lived the South African politics in a very brutal manner. We all did.

There is nothing worse than being forced out of our own home and our family unit dismantled. It is a pain that lasts a lifetime, but I have learnt to live without it dominating my life. You had no choice. Everything you did was for the best; for us. You faced unbearable hardship and went through it. We missed you back home. Both Grandpa and Grandma were worried all the time that we had something to eat, wondering if you had had anything at all.

Everything changed. At school everyone was affected. Even though we played games and did all that we had to do and had done before, I found myself withdrawing. I felt the whole thing so humiliating. The fact that you had had to go to the cities looking for employment was humiliating.

Before the rehabilitation schemes I was always the one with so much love and security and now you were gone. You had been forced by the system of South Africa to leave us.

I travelled from Gudlintaba to Nyaka Primary school daily. I walked six miles each way. At first I walked past our home at Makhanya and now and again I would open doors and windows to let the air in. It was all right for the first few weeks. But then, when I realised the dust that was gathering in, and the fact that it was no use going there to tidy up because you were going to be gone for a long time, and the evidence that the mice had found a breeding ground, I stopped going to the rondavels. The last time was when I opened a suitcase that had yours and Tata's clothes, which you could not take with you, and found that the suitcase had been entered by mice that had left holes on everything in the suitcase. I had looked around the rondavels and in each I found coldness I had never felt before. It was not the coldness of the weather, but that of the energy around.

Slowly as the months went by, the signs of abandonment began to show. The walls showed cracks. The garden had overgrown weeds. At school some children began asking me how long you would be gone. I had no clue and at times we had not received a letter from you and we knew the truth, you had no money, even buying postage stamps and writing paper was a big problem for you, but I told them lies and said you had a good job and I even said that you wrote saying I should visit you. All this was empty talk to play for time with a hope that by the time I was supposedly to visit you I would be gone to another school.

I still made it sound fantastic to them — I mean life in the cities! Just like we had done when we first heard of the rehabilitation schemes. I told them that you were living a far better life than you had done in the village. It was awful. I missed you so much. I suppose, by telling lies to the other children, I did not want to face the truth of your suffering in a place I did not even know and I did not want them to laugh at our family's difficulties.

What I then decided to do was to say very little and did not talk or mix with any of the school children as I had previously done, before the change in the community came. I felt that if I did not talk to them I would reduce the chances of having questions asked about you. You were very special to me, as you still are, and will always be and I had to protect you in the only way I knew how. I became very aloof in your absence. I still did my work excellently just like the way I had done before. But I was feeling so unsure of myself as a person then. I was emotionally insecure. I used to be outgoing and always laughing but all that seemed to have left me when you went away.

I am sure you remember the letters we wrote to you pleading that you should come back. At the time Grandpa Isaac's health was causing concern. He had somehow lost the will to live after getting rid of his livestock and had not even got much money for all what he had had. It was just someone's years of sweat gone down the drain!

Poverty was forced upon people. Moving, having to build a new home especially at his age was awful. Even though both Grandpa and

ESCAPING APARTHEID
A Letter To My Mother

Grandma did not have birth certificates to prove their age, people reckoned Grandpa was about ninety-one in 1959 and Grandma was seventy-six. They looked very healthy and strong as they were always busy working and had enjoyed everything they did. The place Grandpa had marked as his grave, close to that of his mother's, unfortunately had become part of the grazing land. That hurt him very much.

The fact that you were also away, and knowing that you were having a hard time tormented his soul. Every night before we went to bed, they prayed for you to be safe wherever you were and they prayed for you to have a decent shelter. Grandpa called on his mother in the Spirit world to be with you and to protect you all the time. They prayed to God and to their ancestors.

6. YOUR BRIEF RETURN

But when Grandpa was taken seriously ill and we sent you a telegram because he desperately wanted to see you, before he died, as he put it, you came home. We did not even know that you were coming home. I remember very early in the morning a knock on the door while I was making tea for my grandparents. I had just come in from milking the goats as Grandma preferred goat's milk to have in her tea. It was such a shock and joy to see you standing outside the door. You were soaking wet! Do you know that what you did was very brave, because you could have drowned? It had been raining the previous two days.

As you know, the new homes were built on the flat area, at the bottom of Gudlintaba mountain, and further below was Cabane river. This river used to flood frequently and there were times it would flood around our place because of rains in the northern parts of the district. Cabane river used to be difficult to cross at the best of times when there were no rains. Do you remember that you had taken a taxi that dropped you about seven miles away because there were no proper roads for cars to our village, and at the time people tended to use horses as means of transport or just walked?

It was already dark when you got into the taxi at Umzimkhulu town which is about fifteen miles away. You tried to cross Cabane river, flooded as it was, but each time you reached the middle section that used to be very dangerous, you were stopped by some "water animal" that blocked your way, which you described to us as something resembling a dog and each time you turned back. You tried three different sections that you knew very well and of course you were an expert when it came to crossing that river. But at all these sections the doglike animal appeared and blocked your way. After the third time, you decided to sleep on a grassy verge of one of the corn fields along the river. You said you prayed for snakes and scorpions not to come your way while you slept. You were only less than half a mile away from us!

Very early in the morning the water was still high and it was still very dangerous to attempt crossing. But you did it! You took your clothes off except for your knickers and made them into a tiny bundle and secured them to your head with a belt going down and round your back and midriff. You had a suitcase that had a few presents for us. You tried crossing the river with it on your hand but the waves were too forceful and you had to let it go. It was found a week later further down the river caught in some bushes.

The water was up to your shoulders and it was only because you were so determined to see Grandpa that you crossed that river. No one in the village was crossing the river that day.

Everybody was terrified listening to your story. I was so scared! I kept thinking that if you had been swept away by the river, we would not have known and your body might have been found perhaps a week or two later, further down the river or we would not have known it was you if just in case by the time your body was found it was decomposed beyond recognition! Grandpa swore by his dead mother that the animal that you likened to a dog which blocked your way three times was definitely one of his ancestors warning you of the danger, by so doing protecting you!

That day Grandpa ordered that a sheep be slaughtered for your safe return and he said he was thanking his ancestors for looking after you by the river the previous night. It was so good to have you back with us. You nursed Grandpa. Grandma's sad face was replaced by a cheerful smile and her beautiful face looked soft and kind as it used to. We could not go back to Makhanya village because it seemed right you should be the one to look after both Grandpa and Grandma in their last years.

7. NEW JOB, NEW BEGINNING

Now, going back to the end of 1967, I stayed with you until after the new year of 1968 when I went back to Gudlintaba where I stayed with cousin Nombukiso. Both Grandpa and Grandma had died in 1963. I waited for my final results from my Teacher Training College. All final results from various colleges in South Africa were published in newspapers. I had passed and had obtained a distinction in Needlework! All those who had passed had to find out from their district education offices where they would be posted to. Since I trained in the Cape Province, to be precise, in the Transkei, I was going to be posted to a school that had Xhosa as the language. Those who had trained in Natal had to be posted to schools that had Zulu language.

I was posted to Gugwini where I met the father of my children at a local general store one afternoon when I went to buy some vegetables. When I got there he was standing by the counter talking to the shopkeeper and to be honest with you, I did not take notice of him. When I finished paying for my groceries I bid the shopkeeper goodbye and left the shop. On my way home I heard someone calling out from behind: "Hello, Ntomb'entle (Hello beautiful lady)."

I turned and realised that it was the man who had been chatting to the shopkeeper earlier on. He was smiling, saying, "I have not seen someone like you around here before, what is your name and can I accompany you to where ever you are going?"

I told him who I was and that I had just started teaching in the local school. I told him that I was not going to allow a stranger to accompany me. He then told me who he was and then said he would like to visit me when I had time to talk and yes he would introduce himself to my landlady because he did not want her to worry.

I told him I was in a hurry because I had to prepare for the following day's lesson. We parted with him saying that he was sure we would meet again to which I said, "Well, I am sure we will at the general store sometime."

As it turned out, Thami gave me a surprise visit the following afternoon, where I lived. He introduced himself to the owners of the house and asked for their permission to speak to me. My land lady brought him over saying that he had asked for their permission and they did not see any problem because they knew where he lived so they were allowing me to speak to him.

He was very polite to them. When I let him in he said, "I will come to the point and please hear me out. I have been hit by a thunderbolt. When I saw you yesterday, I knew that you were the one for me.

"Over the years I have travelled to many parts of South Africa and have met a lot of people but have not met someone who just blew my mind the way you have done. I could not sleep last night and all day today I have been thinking of you.

"All I am asking is that you give us a chance to talk. I would like to find out about you and I will tell all there is to know about me. How does this sound?"

He told me that he was living at Gugwini under an assumed name of Mahangwana. His real surname was Ngxaliwe and Dumezweni was his great grandfather's name. I agreed that since he had taken the time to come to see me then I would talk to him.

Over the following days he would meet me outside school and we would walk back home together. The school was not far from where I lived but it was still nice to find someone so taken up by me. I enjoyed the attention and within two weeks I was also in love with him.

Thami was a member of Unity Movement, one of South Africa's political movements that were banned because they believed in freedom of opportunity for all regardless of colour and creed. This is the reason he was using an assumed name and living very far from Flagstaff, his own home town.

ESCAPING APARTHEID
A Letter To My Mother

Thami was five foot five, broad shouldered and medium built. He looked strong and had once been interested in boxing and had played rugby. At the beginning he fancied boxing for a living and had taken training at featherweight level. He had a mid dark complexion with thick curly black hair. He smoked a pipe. In fact he was a chain-smoker!

He laughingly joked that smoking a pipe gave him an intellectual and dignified appearance and teased me for my blindness in not seeing those attributes. Thami was the person I used to tell about the situation that faced me at school and how I hated it. He understood and we used to discuss the whole political situation in South Africa, the injustices facing black people.

The political organisation he belonged to wanted to have a system that would benefit all the peoples of South Africa regardless of colour. I suppose because of the anger I had in me which I had had for a number of years, when I met Thami and we talked mostly about things that were politically wrong in South Africa, I wanted change to happen fast. I was very impatient. With him, it felt to me that we were the only people that needed change in that village. The rest were contented with the system. This was how I viewed things and presumed. I was wrong as I later found out.

I was to find out later that there were many good people, uneducated as well as educated who felt just like we did only they did not have to look at those sad faces of children I taught, that confronted me every morning.

I wanted something to happen like yesterday. If I could not change it, I wanted out. I had written to father everything I felt and the Special Branch had taken this as evidence of my dissatisfaction with the system, and also that I was already planning to leave South Africa, so in their eyes and minds I was a very dangerous teacher who was not teaching what I was supposed to teach but going about criticising the system that fed me. So they said.

I knew then that I would never feel free. I never felt free anyway since the rehabilitation schemes.

8. RUNNING AWAY FROM SOUTH AFRICA

This is what I have always wanted you to know: Late June 1968, it was in the evening and dark enough to conceal all suspicious movements when I shook Liz's hand for the last time saying, "Good night and goodbye my friend and remember, you know nothing about my whereabouts."

Liz was a teacher in the same school and had been trained at Sigcawu Teacher Training College as me. We had started at Gugwini Primary School on the same day and as it happened we also rented accommodation in the same household. After my farewell to Liz, I turned and walked cautiously towards a barbed wire fencing I had to creep through to reach an anxiously waiting Thami. My only luggage was a small suitcase with two dresses, a skirt and a pair of shoes, while on the other side of the fence Thami's sole luggage was what he was wearing.

    Creeping through that fence to him knowing that in a few minutes I'd be gone forever brought a feeling of sadness to me. I held his hand and we both sighed with relief knowing that it was a first step towards our freedom. Many hurdles waited ahead; that, we knew for sure. For a split second I turned my head, eyes filled with tears, and stared at the big house I was leaving behind where my landlady slept. I knew deep down in my heart that I would have loved to kiss her cheek for the last time but the situation was such that I should keep her out of it for her own good.

    We walked past all the village houses and huts. The moon was going to come out a bit late. It was a calm night and thankfully the winter winds had kept away, much to our advantage, as it could have been very difficult to walk. It couldn't have been a better night for us considering that we did not have enough clothes to protect us against cold. We did not want to be caught by moonlight within the village in case someone spotted us, so we gathered our pace.

We headed toward the gravel road where one taxi driver within the whole vicinity lived. We were leaving Gugwini village which is in the South East of Umzimkhulu district.

Gugwini village is on a low lying plain and people's homes were scattered around at about 100-200 yards apart or in some instances half to almost a mile apart. The only prominent building in the village was the primary school which at the time was amongst the largest higher primary schools in the district of Umzimkhulu.

I found Gugwini very boring and there was this emptiness about it. Almost dead, even though the local chief's home with many rondavels was close by. It seemed vast and dry looking. No hills, no mountains and no forests around as opposed to the villages I was used to while growing up. After heavy rains the plain low lying areas would be covered with a large number of pools which formed temporary rendezvous. The water was used for mixing soil for making bricks and also for watering gardens. The huts in Gugwini were very different from the ones we had at Makhanya and Gudlintaba in that they seemed to me as though they had been abandoned, no decoration.

If you remember, back in our village the houses (rondavels and four corners) used to be regularly decorated to keep them in good condition. We used to have lovely colours of black and white or any other colours that people chose to use. There were very few homes in Gugwini that looked well off. I suppose it was only the chief, really, who had all the wealth with all his many wives. Of course I remember that because I come from a tribe that is not averse to either bigamy or polygamy.

Thami and I walked as far away from the huts and houses as we possibly could in order to avoid disturbing the dogs but it was not easy. The dogs barked. I was always frightened of dogs but Thami believed in 'barking dogs seldom bite' and urged me to walk as calmly as possible. I tried very hard but I was as terrified as the day when a dog belonging to Miss Ngcobo, our village school teacher at Nyaka, bit

ESCAPING APARTHEID
A Letter To My Mother

my bottom. Do you remember that day? I ran all the way home screaming without delivering the letter you asked me to deliver to Miss Ngcobo. The dog had bitten off a bit of flesh. Since that day I have always been very scared of dogs. I had done what I should not have done for I started running away as soon as the dog started barking. I did not know that was the biggest mistake for the dog started chasing me. I howled with all my vocal chords as it dug its teeth into my bum!

When we had walked about five miles we thought hiring a taxi would help to reduce our journey by a few miles to our first hiding place in the mountains. We decided to go to the taxi driver's house. He lived along the road that ran between Harding and Gugwini but on the direction towards the National Road that led to Umzimkhulu town and the way to Durban and Pietermaritzburg. He was well placed to service both Harding and Umzimkhulu bound passengers.

On approaching his house we were greeted by barking dogs and at that moment a thought that we might have brought ourselves to the Special Branch (SBs) from whom we were running, lingered in my mind. I was terribly scared. Someone came to us carrying a torch and asked what we wanted. We wanted a taxi, we told him. Mr White the taxi owner was not home we were told. We thanked the man and left immediately. I felt relieved in a way for at that time I did not trust anyone. Finding Mr White out on business was our luck as we were to learn later! Back on the gravel road from Mr White's house I said to Thami, "Let's walk faster or better still, can't we run a bit so that we can be far from his house?"

"Why?" Thami asked.

"I am scared and would like to be out of sight before people back there ring the police," I said.

"But running on this road will make things even worse. It will be more revealing. Walk leisurely as though nothing has happened in case someone is watching us — but I know just how you feel. I feel scared myself," said Thami.

We had about fifty-five to sixty miles ahead of us and these we had to cover before sunrise! Although we were terrified it was much better walking on the gravel road leading to the National Road because it was hardly used by vehicles at night. We were in a position to see all vehicles approaching in our direction and we'd have plenty of time to hide by the road side. The problem awaiting us was the National Road which was busy day and night, as a link between every major town, city and province of South Africa. This particular part of the National Road linked Cape Town, Port Elizabeth, East London via Kokstad and Umzimkhulu in the Cape Province to both Durban and Pietermaritzburg in Natal.

There were no signs of any movements among the villages we passed. It was all silence and once in a while a dog barked at a distance. Except for our noises, the silence was broken occasionally by chirruping crickets. There were no more fires lit by the time we joined the National Road, a sign indicating that the villagers were well tucked in their beds, fast asleep.

Only the brightness of the moon lighting the sky together with shining stars were a comfort to us and provided us company. They made our walking much easier. I do not know how and why but they had a comforting effect on me. By the time we left the National Road it was well after midnight. We had by then covered thirty-five miles. We had to climb hills, passing through grassy and rocky paths for another twenty-five miles. It became tougher and rougher as we tried to move faster in order to beat time, which was much against us.

Up and down the hills we went. The moonlight was fast disappearing and it was becoming darker towards dawn. I had no proper walking shoes. I had a pair of low heeled patent shoes. Thami's shoes were better than mine for walking. The strain on my feet was beginning to slow me down and this annoyed me because I was slowing down our progress. My feet were blistering. We had to try and reach our hiding place before sunrise.

We walked past Thembeni, a village where some of the Malunga clan (father's extended family) lived. I saw the church where I was baptised and I thought it would have been nice to bid goodbye to all my relatives instead of passing by in the night and they would never know that I had passed by. I felt sad. I said to Thami how I wished the crickets and the trees could whisper just once to one of the relations that I had passed by at night and gave them all my love. We both laughed at this but it was not a happy laugh — one of sadness.

We were behind schedule as it turned out. By sunrise we still had a long way to go. We were heading for the forest on the mountain facing Thembeni where they were growing wattle trees. Some were being cut while others were being planted. As we walked further up the hill we passed men going to work in some fields. In some areas few tractors were in sight. I was dragging myself by now. My feet were burning with blisters. I was hungry, sleepy, tired and above all feeling very sad. I thought of you.

I had not been allowed to leave Gugwini since the troubles with the Special Branch started. I wanted so much to have been able to tell you everything but they did not allow me, even when I asked for permission to go to Pietermaritzburg to let you know what was happening. They did not think I was being truthful with my request. The truth is, it was true I wanted to see you because I knew sooner or later I would be either put away by them or I would have to escape. I desperately wanted to see you.

We were hungry and tired and had no coins except a cheque which was my month's salary for only R34 (thirty-four rands) and equivalent to about 15 to 17 pound sterling at that time. We had also R5 which we had kept for the taxi. There were no shops around and even if there were, we would not have risked being caught or suspected as runaways by anyone. So we went on slowly and painfully.

We became very short tempered with one another. This was primarily because of hunger, exhaustion, drowsiness, sore feet and yet we knew we had to keep on walking as though we were perfectly all right without any signs that something was wrong with our feet. When the sun rose it shone beautifully over the hills around Thembeni and ahead of us, over the forest we were going to which was also on a mountain. But this meant intolerable heat adding yet another strain on our exhausted bodies.

The problem was we had not been used to walking over the past few months. Had we walked, the distance that we were covering that night was nothing really compared to what we were used to when we lived in the villages. Everybody in the villages walked long distances as part of daily routine.

Anyway, we dragged ourselves with dry lips as we were thirsty and tired. I felt more tired than hungry as we carried on. Every step I made was heavy and very painful. Some of the blisters were weeping and the skin around my heels had completely come off and bleeding. At some point I took the shoes off thinking that it was going to be better walking bare feet as I was used to walking bare feet anyway, but it became more painful as my feet had become used to the shoes I was wearing and the gravel was unbearable on the bare skin. So I put the shoes back on. The mountain we were going to was very close, but with each breath I took and each step, it seemed so far away because I just did not have strength in my body anymore.

It was just after half past ten in the morning when we reached Mr Majola's house. He had been expecting us much earlier. When we entered his house I felt as though a huge load had been removed from my entire body. I wanted to forget all the troubles surrounding us — just for a few hours. All I needed was a bath, food and sleep. I was meeting him and his beautiful girlfriend for the first time. They were very hospitable and kind and also very brave for they were helping us, people running away from the government agencies while they were working as government employees in the plantation programme. Majola was twenty-eight years old, the same age as Thami. He was about five-feet-nine, tall and slim, with a dark complexion and short black hair. He had a laid back manner and was softly spoken with a kind face and a constant smile in his brown eyes.

His girlfriend was called Khwezi (Star). Khwezi shortened for Nomakhwezi. They were both Xhosas. Khwezi was the same height as me, five-feet-six. She was a bit plump but with an outgoing personality. She just lit up the room with her whole being as soon as she walked in. Her complexion was fair with a very smooth skin. She had her black hair in neat plaits and it had a thick texture that I admired. She was very pretty. She helped me to the bathroom by supporting me gently as I could hardly walk by then.

She ran the bath for me and told me to "...just lie in there and enjoy every bit at this moment for you do not know what the road ahead is going to be like, Sisi (sister), and when you are done, call me if you still need me to support you back to the sitting room."

With that she smiled but with a sympathetic look in her eyes. She also said that she would bring me something to wear. "It is best that the clothes you had on, be washed today and I will wash them with the rest of the washing I am doing for me and Majola." I thanked her deeply for her kindness.

9. TATA AND THAMI

The bath was soothing. I felt grateful that the first people who were helping us were kind and very understanding. I thought it was a good sign that meant the South African Special Branch were not going to get us. With this in mind I became strong and very determined that I would survive whatever was thrown at me. I got out of the bath a bit unsteady on my feet which were still sore. But I felt revived and knew that I would make it on my own without Khwezi's support to the sitting room. Khwezi's dress was comfortable and a bit baggy.

In the sitting room Thami's face lit up when he saw me walk in and he was very proud of me. He told Majola that I was his strength and I had been through a very difficult time with the Special Branch. Majola asked me then what my family name was. When I told him that it was 'Malunga', his face momentarily froze and he quickly asked me if I knew an elderly man called Sheldrake Malunga. I told him that the elderly man was my grandfather as he was my grandfather's brother, meaning he was my father's uncle.

Majola then said, "Well you will have to stay indoors all the time you are here because Tat'Malunga will not be happy with you or any of us."

"Does he know you, Thami? No I do not think so. No man in his mind will allow their grand daughter to run away with a man they hardly know! He will not want to know that you are running away and planning on leaving South Africa. Tat'Malunga (father Malunga) is working here with us as the foreman."

"How sad and cruel is this situation?" I said. He is my only surviving grand father and he is very loving. I wish I could see him but I know I cannot for both our sakes."

Thami agreed with both Majola and I, cursing under his breath, the South African system that broke families. Khwezi prepared

ESCAPING APARTHEID
A Letter To My Mother

oat porridge for my breakfast after which I went to sleep.

It was late in the afternoon when I woke up. It was a Friday. We had left on a Thursday evening at about six. Back at school there would be chaos with my absence. I lay awake and reflected painfully on the events which prevailed over the past weeks and had led us where we were. I thought of that Tuesday evening in May 1968 at my landlady's home, when everything turned upside down! All day I had been very cheerful and happy, entertaining my father, my landlord, Thami and four more villagers, one of whom was Thami's distant brother-in-law. We had not been to school because it had been a bank holiday. It had been a lovely sunny day. We had gone to Harding town in the morning with both father and Thami and had returned to my place where I had prepared a meal and then they had drinks which they had bought from Harding.

Tata had come visiting me from Pietermaritzburg. I had written to him to ask for his permission to allow me to leave South Africa. I had also sent him a form which he had to sign in order that I could obtain a travel document to Swaziland. I wanted to go and teach in Swaziland instead of South Africa, in the Transkei. I know Tata did not tell you about that letter for he feared that you would worry a lot. I had not told you that I wanted to leave teaching in the Transkei because I did not want to upset you but I hoped that once Tata had given me the permission or rather understood my predicament, he would speak to you and explain more to you and make you understand why I had decided that I did not want to teach at Gugwini. But Tata had come down from Pietermaritzburg to persuade me to change my mind and stay in the Transkei instead.

He worried about the fact that since he had burnt his 'dom pas' early in the sixties, he had been unable to get long term jobs because he needed to produce an identity card each time he went for a job, and he did not intend on getting one because he felt very strongly against these identity cards.

Tata was torn apart emotionally. He hated to see you work endless hours to support the family and yet even at times when he thought of going to apply for it, he would not have been able to raise enough money for the fines that would have been imposed on him for having had no 'dom pas' for a number of years since their introduction.

It was humiliating for him to go on without a stable job. It was humiliating also for him to carry the 'dom pas'. He said he was born and bred in South Africa and did not want to submit to the horrible system of South Africa's Apartheid which meant that he did not exist, and to prove his existence for the whites, he had to carry a pass. He said that he would not do this as long as he lived.

It was such a personal thing for him, something that tore at the core of his manhood. The fact that he was not the only black person being forced to carry the 'dom pas', did not make him feel any better. Father never told you that he hated the system so much. He just kept saying that he did not have enough money because he was having a problem getting a job.

He also said that going to the authorities, applying for 'dom pas' would definitely land him in prison for non possession of it. So he was prepared to go on as long as it took, dodging the law and getting odd jobs here and there. He did not like it, but that was what he was going to do until the day he died.

Tata also told me that he had found a Herbal College where he was able to study and also had found a qualified Herbalist willing to take him on and teach him while he was also studying at the College. He did not have to attend the College every day, he attended once a week and spent more time with the qualified Herbalist and that way, he was gaining a lot of practical knowledge. He said he wanted to be a healer and was very passionate about this when he told me. He also said it would take a number of years before he properly qualified.

With the odd jobs he had managed to fund his studies but it was hard going. He told me that he came to stop me from leaving South Africa for Swaziland because with my job I would be able to relieve you from the hardship, as I could help you financially. Tata really wanted me to stay and assist you.

On that May afternoon at about four o'clock, while Tata and the other men including Thami were drinking and discussing politics, we saw a white four door saloon Ford Escort driving past our house. Since there was so much laughter coming from the rondavel, the men did not take notice of the car. They were having a good time with their drinks and discussions. The car drove past the school where I taught towards the local chief's home. Gugwini village had very few vehicles and to see one, especially on a holiday, was a matter of curiosity for us women. Liz, suggested that it was perhaps one of the chief's daughter's visitors. I agreed with her. Thirty minutes later the same car drove past our place again and I did not think of it until late that evening.

When it became dark at around 5:30, Tata and the men decided to disperse. He accompanied Thami and Thami's brother-in-law back to their house. Tata was to leave for Pietermaritzburg the following day, which was Wednesday. They had not gone long when I heard them coming back, and judging from their footsteps I could tell that something interesting and exciting was happening. They rushed in, Tata and Thami. The only words I heard as they came in was "It's hot my girl!" I knew what they meant.

Thami's brother-in-law had gone to his house where the white Ford Escort was waiting. They had decided that he should go in to find out how bad the situation was. What had alerted them as they approached the house, were torches with flashing lights. They heard voices which were unfamiliar and the car had been parked in a suspicious manner, as if whoever parked it did not want it to be seen.

Tata and Thami came back to warn me of the situation. At that moment I had to take charge, and I somehow got the courage.

We left the rondavel and walked out of the yard and stood about a hundred yards from the house, beside a rose bush which was shadowed from the houses around. This gave us a few minutes to watch the SBs as they approached our place, now accompanied by Thami's brother-in-law.

By this time the moon had just come out and was shining brightly. The sky was blue, not a single cloud except the shining stars. Our calculation was that the SBs were looking for Thami and therefore they would not waste time but come over to my place looking for him, after asking his brother-in-law. Indeed this was so.

Fortunately for us, they went to the wrong house as we watched them and this gave us time to exchange a few words and I immediately rushed back to my room after biding both Tata and Thami goodbye. At that point I did not even know what was going to happen and when I would see both of them, if at all.

I had not been in long when there was banging at the door. There were three whites, one coloured with a very white complexion, and one black. Thami's brother-in-law was told to go back home. By the looks on their faces I sensed immediately that it was going to be rough. When I looked at their shining faces and hefty bodies I felt anger. It was anger that was generated by a few things and thoughts: a few yards or miles away from where these men stood, in those houses and huts around the village of Gugwini, slept people who were suffering from malnutrition.

We had both experienced suffering from rehabilitation schemes, poverty that was forced upon us in the form of slums of

Pietermaritzburg. I thought of Linda, my lovely nephew, and the words I had scribbled as a tribute to him which went like this:

Linda I loved you.
You were such a pretty boy.
Your dark ebony face,
smooth and shiny.
Beautiful big brown eyes
ever sparkling
In a face ever smiling.
But you died
A painful death my love.

You were only three.
You could not understand
What was eating you.
Your young body, needed
All that's needed
For a young body to grow.

But because of poverty
And a system that's cruel
In the Republic of South Africa
And for what we are — black
You died, Linda.

ESCAPING APARTHEID
A Letter To My Mother

I cried bitterly the day I returned
From College to find you untouchable.

You came close and touched me and smiled, Linda.
You were moving slowly with death in you.
You were a victim of malnutrition.
In a country that's very wealthy
A country of Gold and Diamonds
Where our black folks dig in mines
Boosting South Africa's economy.

It was not only you Linda.
Many kids were dying.
But you were too close to my heart.
Our families could only provide
Maize porridge for your survival
Which did not help you at all.
We were helpless, Linda.

The swelling.
The skin as if it had been burnt
A slight touch causing it to come off —
Oh Linda what you went through!
You had to die — in Edendale.
It was in 1966.

NOMANONO ISAACS

Kwashiorkor killed you my love.
Malnutrition – in a beautiful,
Wealthy, Sunny South Africa.
A paradise for the white man.

10. AN EVENING WITH SPECIAL BRANCH

I decided there and then that I was not going to be used by the SBs against Thami or Tata. I was not going to assist them in any way in order to arrest Tata and Thami. The Special Branch police officers asked me where Thami and Tata were. I told them that they had gone to town to look for some more beer. I was asked several times why Thami and Tata had decided to go so far at that time of night. My answer was "Harding is the only nearest place where they can buy beer." Amongst the SBs I immediately recognised who was going to give me a hard time and who was not. The coloured one was the meanest of all.

He spoke very good Xhosa. He spoke more than the rest of them. He seemed like their champion in interrogations. What also made my resolve to do all I could to save Tata and Thami, was the fact that the black man with them was treated no better than me. They called him Vatteman (fat man). He was actually fat. Even though they pretended that he was one of them, it was obvious that to them he was just another 'kaffir'. He talked to me with the same authority as the whites and the coloured but when talking to them, he would not be any different from a garden boy speaking to his madam.

He would say timidly and obediently, Ja Baas, Nie Baas (Yes Boss, No Boss). I felt this was very humiliating for him in front of me. To him I suppose it was routine, something he was doing every day in his job. I just felt sorry and angry for him. He of course did not need me to feel sorry for him or angry for him for that matter. It was just the hopelessness of the situation he was in. That of an authority to me but his authority did not go any further than just trying to impress his bosses on how good he was at swearing, trying to break me with insults together with his counterpart, the coloured.

Those two swore at me all the time they talked and asked questions. But the more they swore, the more I got determined that I was not going to give in.

Two of the whites were patient. But the third had a hard time trying to suppress his anger and he would frequently go very red, his nostrils twitching and his eyes would look at me as though they wanted to kill. He did not need to talk to me. He just looked at me with so much contempt and his face red all the while!

The two that swore at me were used by the other two who gave the impression of being patient. They emptied my suitcase by throwing everything on to the floor and just leaving everything in a mess. They took everything that was paper including my family photographs. That hurt me a lot. They threw my clothes on to the floor.

You see, I did not have any other clothes except what you had got me while I was at Teacher Training College and I still intended to keep them for a while. Do you know what one of the white men said as he threw my clothes and the suitcase on the floor? He laughingly said, "These are the only clothes you have in your suitcase — you are a teacher you should have more than a few rags." To that I laughed. It was not because I liked what he said but because he did not know what he was saying and why I had so few rags, and yet I was a teacher.

Of course as whites they had everything. They had a better life. They never had rags in their houses. They had better wages and salaries. All these things were determined when they were born because of the colour of their skins. My fate was also determined on the day I was born, because of the colour of my skin. That I would struggle for life and have those few rags and listen to him abusing me and my people, treating us far worse than the life of slugs!

The white system of South Africa had made sure that I remained where I was without any choice to what I wanted to study or what I wanted to be.

The white officer had a choice. His children had a choice. So I laughed because of so many things that he was deliberately naïve

ESCAPING APARTHEID
A Letter To My Mother

about. Unfortunately Thami's documents were with me. I had just finished reading what he was writing. Some letters I had written without posting to father criticising the system of Bantu Education were taken. You realise that the education we had under the Bantu Education system was inferior. We did not have much choice. For girls it was either teacher training or nursing. I mean those from struggling families like ours. Those from well-to-do families could become lawyers and doctors but that meant a lot of money.

Do you remember that I wanted to be a nurse and you talked me against it, wanting me to be a teacher instead? At that time I was sure that what I wanted to do was nursing and I did not want to go to Teacher Training at all. As a result, my first year at Sigcawu Teacher Training College was very bad; that is, the first half of the year.

I had started late because there was a problem about who was going to finance my entire teacher training programme. My former headmaster at Mfulamhle Higher Primary School, Mr Mokoena agreed to pay for my fees on the understanding that I would pay him back once I had qualified and had a job. It was noble of him to do that for me. I am grateful and will always be grateful to him and his family.

I must say however, that this was a common practice in the district of Umzimkhulu as far as I remember, for people who could afford a little more to be asked to finance education for those who were unable to. Most people got educated this way.

It was during the June holidays, half year holidays, when I was back at Umzimkhulu living with cousin Nombukiso that I had time to analyse my feelings. I had done absolutely nothing at college during the first two terms and had returned early because the previous two months before the end of term I was bed ridden suffering from mumps and had been in isolation for the two months and had done no work at all.

I know that the fact that I was training for teaching, and still felt that I should have gone for nursing instead, was dominating my mind, affected my work and my health. During the holidays when I had recovered I decided to get hold of myself. I thought of the suffering that you were going through from the horrible underpaid jobs you were doing just to survive in Pietermaritzburg. It was difficult enough to keep yourself and my young brothers.

I felt I was wasting valuable time and throwing an opportunity of ever being in a position to help the family so you could stop all the jobs you were doing. So I went back to college determined to do very well. I knew that I was able to learn quickly once I had set my mind. There were around eleven subjects we had to do and I had to start from the beginning. I had only three months left in the first year.

Do you remember what I did? I even surprised myself and the college staff could not believe it. My classmates were amazed. I had come last and had done absolutely no work at the beginning of the year and on top of that I had arrived in March when I should have arrived in January for the beginning of the term. Since I had had to leave college just before the end of May, I now had only August to October to do my course work.

In November we were sitting for the examinations. Everyone expected me to fail. That did not bother me because I knew my strengths and I was not going to fail. I had never failed any class in all the years and I was not going to begin at Teacher Training College. The thought of going home at the end of the year having failed my first year at college frightened me. I turned my results round. I had come last the previous term and this time I came third and that pleased me and surprised me a little. There were around sixty students overall in our year.

With those results, I had proved a point to myself that I could do the training and that I could learn to like teaching. I decided to like teaching. But as it turned out, I was never able to relieve you of your struggle after all that and for all I know, your life today, twenty-four years on from the time I qualified with the intention of helping you, your struggles are still continuing. I feel sad and responsible for all the suffering you have endured since then.

I live with tremendous guilt, that, had I not left and had I not got bothered with the political set up, I would have been able to look

ESCAPING APARTHEID
A Letter To My Mother

after you. I would have continued teaching, at least earning a living, however meagre, I don't know. But there are those times when I believe that I would have gone away somehow, teaching in the neighbouring countries instead of the Transkei. I also feel very strongly that I would have ended up in jail anyway because I would have found teaching under those conditions—that system—very difficult.

I would have found it difficult to keep my mouth shut as we were expected to as teachers. What I know is that, we all never really know what life holds for us. Not even the next hour, let alone tomorrow.

In the rondavel with the Special Branch officers, Tata's shaving kit bag was hanging by its strap on the back rest of a chair. It was a small leather bag. It was opened and everything turned out to be uninteresting — razor blades foaming brush, etc. I was asked how they travelled to Harding then I remembered the white car which had passed in front of our home. I knew then that it was the very car the SBs were travelling in and I described a car to them, describing their very own.

I had nothing else to say that would reduce the pressure put on me. I had to say something. At one point I had four people asking different questions and on top of that these were accompanied by insults and sarcastic remarks.

There's just one thing that I found very humiliating—I had not had enough time to dress properly before they came in.

When Tata left accompanying the other men, I had a wash and I was half dressed when they came rushing back with Thami. I just put on a skirt and a dressing gown on top without having time to put on underwear. Having gone to the rose bush in a hurry with them and rushing back into the room before the SBs came in, I only had time for taking the washing basin and throwing the water out. So all the time I was being questioned I had no knickers on.

When the owners of the place came and knocked at the door (I knew they hurt for me) to ask if everything was all right, they were both dismissed indignantly and I felt very angry and felt more determined that I was not going to be used by the South African police, black or white, come what may. I felt that they could have told these old people in a polite manner. Instead they were dismissed in a humiliating way. These were my elders and to have them treated in that horrible way hurt me. They had not done anything wrong but had wanted as the owners of the place to know what was going on. They had a right to know, I felt.

One of the SBs suggested that we drive to Harding which is roughly ten miles away to the west of Gugwini. The purpose was to check on all the cars in town. It was not a big town but big enough to exhaust me by going round and round to all car parks and all over the streets of Harding trying to locate the car that supposedly had given a lift to both Tata and Thami.

Of course we never found the car. They were very angry and cold. I was cold too. But they were better dressed for winter than I was. They had not allowed me to put on my knickers when I requested to before we went to Harding. The answer I had received from one of them was that there was no need to wear knickers because I was behaving no better than a tart and therefore there was nothing to protect underneath there, as they put it, as they assumed that I was no longer a virgin, something that they knew I had to keep as part of my custom, until after the wedding day. They knew all our customs and they knew that saying things like that would hurt and humiliate me more because, as you know, it is expected that a girl will remain a virgin until the day she gets married. All what they were doing were trying to break me.

    Towards midnight we drove back to my place. All the driving was done in darkness. They did not switch their headlights on. Their aim was not to give themselves away should someone see the car from a long distance away. On arrival I was not allowed back into the house. By the way, when we drove to Harding, Vatteman (the black SB) had been left behind to look out for Tata and Thami. On our return they only checked the padlock at the door and found it still locked. They never bothered to go in.

ESCAPING APARTHEID
A Letter To My Mother

We all remained in the car. They slept in turns guarding me and whenever I happened to be dozing I was awakened by insults from either Vatteman or the coloured. It would be improper of me to actually repeat the things that they said as insults.

You know how we were taught and brought up never to swear; especially girls were seen as of low character if they swore. So you can imagine how bad I felt when they continued to insult me, humiliating and questioning my morality as a girl in that part of the world where values, that is, women had to behave in certain ways to show that they were of good character.

I took those insults very personally. For them to insinuate that I was no longer a virgin hurt me to the core of my soul. They told me that as a teacher in South Africa—Transkei—I was going to be taken away and the penalty for assisting or even associating with people who were questioning the system, which was the government that was employing me, paying my salary, they told me, I was liable to three years in prison.

And they asked if I had ever heard of Robben Island and when I told them that I had heard of it, they said they were sure that I would not like to have Robben Island as my home for the following three years, as I would be sent there if I did not co-operate with them. I felt then that life for me in South Africa was not going to be pleasant whatever I did. I did not want to be used by them. The threats of being sent to Robben Island did not scare me.

At around three in the morning I was asked what I thought had happened to my father. Why he had not returned from town. I told them that I suspected that they had returned when we were looking for the car in Harding and they had realised from the mess of the clothes and papers which were scattered in the room that the SBs had been in. They must have then decided to run away.

When I said this they all rushed out of the car in a suppressed state of panic and went to the house. This time they unlocked the padlock which was still left the way it had been, only to find that they had already wasted time for my father's bag and Thami's jacket were gone.

ESCAPING APARTHEID
A Letter To My Mother

Later I was to learn from Thami that Vatteman had seen them returning, as he had been left behind. He had been given a revolver and I wondered why he did not arrest them. They had walked past him standing about fifty yards from the fence that was only four yards away from the house. Tata and Thami had watched the house from the rose bush and had seen the car leave. Our assumption was that Vatteman was not sure of what would happen to his life—perhaps he thought that they were armed, as he was, and thought that perhaps they would resist arrest and so he had decided to play it cool and close his eyes while on the look-out. On the other hand, he must have just decided to let them go. Nobody knew what went on in his mind and why he did not arrest them.

My task then at that time of early morning was to go with them (SBs) all the way to Umzimkhulu, the nearest town on the Cape Province—bordering Natal—where father could get transport to Natal.

Umzimkhulu town, as the border town between Natal and the Cape, would have been the right place, under normal circumstances, to wait for transport to Pietermaritzburg as there were plenty of taxis, licensed as well as pirates. But this time the SBs underestimated both Tata and Thami.

There was no way Tata would have gone to Umzimkhulu to wait for transportation. He was a very tough walker and he knew the area very well, almost inside out. Driving so early in the morning to Umzimkhulu town with a hope that Tata would be sleeping in one of the waiting rooms, as the SBs said, sounded ridiculous to me, but I had to follow the instructions. The SBs, especially, white men, knew everything. Their way of thinking far exceeded mine to have common sense!

The other thing they did not know was that I was not going to point a finger at my own flesh and blood. I was not going to point my finger to any of them. But the SBs thought because they gave me the instruction and I was black, I would do as they wanted. I was not going to identify them to be arrested and be detained without trial. The system in South Africa did not treat blacks as worthy of decent living and rights, so it was my right to do as I

ESCAPING APARTHEID
A Letter To My Mother

felt and not as I was told by them. At that moment, I felt I had the power.

For a short while, I did not know for how long my power was going to last, but I did not care, I wanted to do as I felt. Those white men, depended on me to make their white domination system continue. I felt good about this. Both Tata and Thami belonged to political organisations which were banned by the South African government, and according to the SBs, they were going to encourage terrorism which I knew very well was not the case. They were personally against violence.

At Umzimkhulu there was no sign of life as everyone was fast asleep. Only one man with his fire, a night watchman, sat at the corner of Barclays Bank and Madonela Supermarket. It was a cold night but that old man had to sit there guarding the interests of 'our bosses' while they slept comfortably in their beds. Nobody cared whether he died while on duty for he was dressed in flimsy clothing not suitable for a cold May night.

He had a baton and an unloaded hunting gun beside him. He looked a pathetic figure that could absolutely do nothing if he had been attacked by robbers! We went to the bus rank. The door was unceremoniously pushed open in the waiting room and the men in there had their sleep disturbed. People slept on concrete floors. There was no heating. It was very cold. A few people had blankets but the rest had used their jackets just to cover the upper parts of their bodies. These were men going to board a bus the following morning, on their way to different mines in the Transvaal and the Orange Free State. It was always easy to tell who was going to the mines in those waiting rooms of Umzimkhulu town.

The SBs when pushing the doors open seemed to me as though they took all the people sleeping on the concrete floors for mere creatures no better than goats in a kraal. I had to say Yes or No as they went around pulling blankets off those people's faces in order to find my father and Thami. They were not there of course. We left the waiting room banging the door behind us.

Everybody was hungry now. The car was driven towards the night watchman and parked. Someone took out a kettle from the boot and went to a nearby tap to fill it.

ESCAPING APARTHEID
A Letter To My Mother

They directed the night watchman—who immediately, seeing white men, stood up and saluted as if he was in the army, a sign of respect for a white man, by someone who did the type of job the old man was doing; that is, in some parts of South Africa—to boil the kettle for them on his open fire. They made coffee and brought it to the car. They took out cheese and biltong (dried raw meat).

I watched with interest and amusement as they drank their coffee eating cheese and biltong, for although Vatteman behaved with so much superiority when addressing me in the presence of his bosses, his tumble was packed separately from those of his colleagues, which were together. He did not even share the cheese and biltong in the way the others shared. He was only given what was left over after the others had enthusiastically and greedily eaten. What he got were very few bits of cheese and tiny strings of biltong.

Each time these crumbs were passed onto him he eagerly and obediently said, "Dankie Meneer" — "Thank you Sir" like a very grateful child who'd had a very pleasant surprise! He was black, just as I am. Whatever his job was, they could not share food with a black colleague, which in fact I doubt if they even in their wildest dreams ever considered him a colleague.

Somehow I felt sorry for him. I don't know why, but I did. Even though he had insulted me so much and hurt me so, I just felt he had to try harder to impress his bosses.

I just got more and more determined after seeing the way they treated him during their feast – if one could call it that! There was no way that I would let them hear from my own lips these words, "that is father, that is Thami."

I hated Vatteman for having sworn at me but yet I felt sorry for him for having been treated in that manner in my presence. Of course to his bosses there was nothing amiss, it was routine. Even to Vatteman this was his life in that job and it would remain that way. He did not know any difference. I am convinced that in his own way, he must have felt very important in my presence being given cheese and biltong (even though they were crumbs) by these white men while I watched them all. The fact that he ate these things he couldn't really afford in his house I am sure made him feel great and gave him a superiority feeling towards me. Yet his treatment in my presence, indicated that he was just another 'kaffir'.

I was hungry but I concentrated on how best to remain safe and to appear as co-operative as possible. I knew that as soon as they finished eating, they would fire various questions at me. I had to come up with answers very quickly because when I hesitated they immediately said I was telling a lie and they became nasty. Even though I had been mentally preparing myself for their questions, when they finished eating, one of them turned to me with such contempt and nastiness in his voice demanding that I tell them where Tata and Thami were. Because of the tone of his voice, I became angry and told him that I did not know anymore and I did not answer his questions anymore and this made him very angry. I kept silent until he exhausted himself and the others spoke to him in Afrikaans telling him to calm down and leave me for a while.

Then it was another drive back to Gugwini. It was just before sunrise now. It was their last attempt to see if anyone had returned. They also told me that we were going to Pietermaritzburg, which was between hundred and hundred and twenty miles away. I then asked for permission to tell my landlady that I wasn't going to be home and to ask her to report my absence to my headmaster. They told me that I had no right to talk to anyone while I was with them. So one of them went and talked to my landlord.

Off we went, not straight to Pietermaritzburg but first to Kokstad, which was approximately sixty to seventy miles to the north west of Gugwini. At Kokstad Thami's belongings, which had been collected from his brother-in-law's house, were left together with other documents and literature which was in fact banned in South Africa.

Driving to Kokstad reminded me of the journeys I frequently had going to Sigcawu Teacher Training College in Flagstaff. Mine were long and exhausting because I used buses from Umzimkhulu and changed at Kokstad to get a bus to Flagstaff and would get off just before Flagstaff town and walk down a hill to College. But this particular day was different. I was in a very comfortable car but I was not at all enjoying the trip for I did not know what my future was going to be at that point.

11. ROAD TRIP

I tried to take in the scenery as the car was driven at a very high speed towards Kokstad. At that speed, the trees that lined the National Road seemed to be passing by at a terrific speed as I could hardly feel the movement of the car—it was very, very comfortable. You know what I mean.

Most people in the villages that we drove past were just getting up. There was smoke in houses that stretched on the hills along the route. In some places there were people getting their livestock out of the kraals and others were milking cows and goats. There were also those car convoys that used to travel between Cape Town and Durban of newly manufactured cars. I found myself counting the cars in the convoys as we drove past, on the opposite direction as they were Natal bound. This counting was to be the pattern all day long for me. If I was not counting the cars in convoys, I would be counting the road markings and working out the distance between the different road signs.

That day I found myself learning the highway code which I had never known. Observing the driving and what cars did according to the signs on the roads as we drove along, I felt good that I had learnt something even though I knew that I could never drive in South Africa, or anywhere in the world for that matter, as I thought I would spend my life in South African jails and probably die in one of those jails like so many black prisoners had under suspicious circumstances.

Cars were not for the likes of us in that poverty, I thought. As I was not allowed to sleep the counting helped me to keep awake. The SBs thought father would be the easier to get hold of and they thought if they found him, he would tell them where Thami was. As we drove from Kokstad heading eastwards to

ESCAPING APARTHEID
A Letter To My Mother

Pietermaritzburg, at yet another high speed, the group split into two. I was with two white SBs. The other three went in another car. Both cars left Kokstad at around seven in the morning and headed towards Umzimkhulu.

The car I was in was in front and we parted ways with the other one at the junction to Harding which was the same as the route to Gugwini. At that point I did not know why the other car headed back to Gugwini but I was to learn years later what happened at Gugwini that day.

The weather was lovely that Friday morning. As we drove towards Umzimkhulu past Clydesdale parish I thought of the days I had spent there studying for my Junior Certificate (Secondary Education). I thought of all the people I had known while I attended the Secondary School there.

The first impression of the area—that of a very crowded village. It was not a village but I was used to villages and had never seen a place like Clydesdale before. This was a place where most wealthy people as far as I was concerned lived. It was a prosperous place and to go to

Clydesdale Secondary School was a prestigious thing indeed. It was a place where blacks and coloureds lived before the coloureds where moved out to 'coloureds only places'. They were rehabilitated in places around Cape Town and Port Elizabeth, we were told. Whether this was the case or not we were never sure.

What I remember is that it was a very depressing time for most people at Clydesdale, especially for those coloureds who did not want to move. There were those, of course, who felt that their status was far better than that of blacks so they were happy to move because they felt that they would be moving to better places and their lives would improve. They would be just a fraction closer to the white status!

Students attending Clydesdale Secondary School came from various parts of the Umzimkhulu District. All of us had to ask families around the parish to keep us and to earn our stay we had to contribute by doing various chores. As we drove past Clydesdale, now very close to Umzimkhulu town, say about a mile, I was reminded of my own days when I used to walk the National Road every other Friday afternoon going back to the village of Gudlintaba. We used to travel in groups and the journey was made easy that way.

There was, this particular morning, scores of young people making their way to Clydesdale Secondary School. I wondered what my old teachers at the Secondary School would say that morning if they were to see me with the Special Branch, because I was always obedient and one of their best students. I did everything I was required to do and obeyed the College rules. But they had never known of the deep feelings I had while growing up in the villages.

Having qualified at Sigcawu Teacher Training College and taken a teaching post at Gugwini, where there were so many poor children, just made me feel so bad each morning going to school. It felt like I was reliving my family hardships through the eyes of those children. In them I saw the struggles you were continuously going through to make ends meet in order to support all of us.

Gugwini High School was large so it also had a primary school which is the area I worked at. There were about forty children in each class and in some cases there were more, and that meant splitting a class in two sections. I was given the ten to eleven age group but as you know, the ages of children tended to be ignored so we had children older than that attending classes for this particular age group because some of them had missed school due to financial problems their families had.

What faced me as the initial problem was the class room. It was a rondavel with thatching that was fast deteriorating. There were gaps in the thatch that were all right on warm days but on cold and windy days, the papers were constantly being blown around the class room. The children were freezing cold and so was I.

It was very difficult to concentrate on any work. There was nothing the headmaster could do because of the shortage of money. On top of this, these children did not have adequate clothing for winter conditions. There was no way of arranging any form of heating. The children came from very poor families. It was heartbreaking. Their parents could not afford to feed them let alone to pay for the required school fees. They walked bare feet on cold and frosty mornings coming to cold, dusty classrooms. They were dusty because of the gaping holes on the thatched roofs and the winds that blew left the desks and floors covered in dust.

The school regulation was that if a child did not buy books and had not paid any fees, which in most cases they could not afford, the child had to be sent home. Most of them looked very tired and hungry because they came to school having had nothing to eat. But when I asked if they had eaten they always said yes. I knew they were only saying that because of their family pride. I had always said the same thing when I was their age. It was embarrassing to tell strangers of your own home circumstances. Above all, it was a sense of retaining some form of dignity.

I felt bad each time I had to ask them to bring money to buy books because I knew they were not going to bring any money. What I could not face was asking them to go back home. It was a regulation that after a certain period children who had not bought books should be sent home in order for their parents to realise the importance of providing money to purchase all the relevant books. That I could not do and did not do.

I put myself in a very difficult situation because there were no books for them to share. The school did not provide any. But children in those circumstances were very understanding. Those that had books used to share with those who did not have them. But this was not enough because there were more that did not have them.

The months of May, June and July are the coldest as you know. Now imagine attempting to teach children in a very cold class room with wind blowing through the roof, children who did not have warm clothes on, on bare feet, hungry and who sat there looking at you in a helpless gaze.

It was sad and very heartbreaking for I had to pretend that it was not that bad and carried on the best I could. I had no authority to send them back home on very cold days to the warmth of their poverty stricken homes. They would have been a lot warmer back in their homes with open fires even though they would be hungry. The classroom we had was in a dilapidated state. Our headmaster, Godlo Mgingqizana, did not even bother to come to the section we were in. He did not know what we were going through.

They just stared with very sad eyes. They did not smile much. I was reminded so much of my own school days and realised that things had not changed and they were not going to change for a very, very long time. I hated going to work every morning for the children's sad eyes, were a constant torment to me. The helplessness of the situation pained me all the time.

Most children in the group I had could not read nor write properly because of the automatic promotion system that had been introduced in recent years. Most of the kids had had hard times financially over the years, which had made starting school almost impossible for their families. They had never had books of their own. Nothing really. They had been just pushed along to the next class. I was questioning a lot of things.

I could not understand why other teachers had turned a blind eye to these children's problems and just pushed them to the next year knowing that they had not learnt anything. The education system was bad. But I felt that the school could have done something about it.

They could have found a way round the problem. They could have tried harder to assist the children who were the victims of the system. But on the other hand the teachers themselves had a lot to cope with. The numbers in classes for a start were more than it is possible to give individual attention to any child. There were many subjects that the teachers had to teach and were faced with so few resources.

The pressures around everyone were a lot. At that time I did not see the teachers' side; that is, those who had previously taught the children I then had. I just felt the children had been let down by the teachers themselves. I felt that they could have given intensive, special extra time to the children from the beginning so that at least they could be reading and writing properly at the age of ten and eleven. I was a very angry young teacher. I was angry with the debasing education system itself, the South African racist Apartheid system and very angry with the very school that I was now teaching at.

The children were being cheated of education and I was becoming part of the system that was not helping the children at all. I did not like to be part of it.

It was nothing to do with the fact that I had never wanted to be a teacher. No, I was looking forward to teaching by the time I completed my training programme, after talking to myself and working hard to get good grades at Teacher Training College, you remember that?

It was the fact that I was reliving my own childhood pains back then after the rehabilitation schemes when poverty had been forced upon us. I knew and understood the hurt and pain the parents of the children were going through having to see their children returned from school for lack of money. I felt the pain the children were feeling, a feeling of unworthiness because they did not have books and the uniforms that other children had.

They had come to school having had nothing to eat. The parents had sent them with a hope that perhaps by the time they got back home in the evening they would have been able to find some money or food somehow to give them something to eat.

Yes, I was seeing and looking from the outside and yet experiencing the pain perhaps more then because I felt I had now become part of the horrible system, that of authority to the children and their parents. I had to do what I did not believe in. How could I honestly send a child home for not having a proper uniform when that child did not have the most essential things—food and books? What they came wearing in my class were old clothes. Rags. I was no better than them myself. The white man had been right when he said that all I had were mere rags. What he did not know though was that I was very proud of my rags because they came to me from LOVE! Your love, and THANK YOU!

This was the reason therefore that I wrote a letter to Tata asking him for permission to let me go teach in Swaziland. I wanted out of South Africa. I had never left South Africa before. I had this romantic idea in my mind that things or teaching conditions in Swaziland as an Independent State would be all right. It was a multiracial state too, so I thought things would certainly be good. I could not just resign. I had to get a travel document first and then apply for a teaching job. I had to have father's signature because I was under twenty-one years old.

The letter that the SBs took was to Tata with all the grievances about the education system. The unfairness in the whole country, the children in the school and how I felt about the whole lot. The unspoken suffering mirrored in the eyes of those children. I can still see it as I write this so many years on. I did not want to be part of the cruel system. I felt used, someone to inflict more hurt and more pain by being a teacher under those conditions.

I could not just go on with the way things were. At the end of the year when I had so many problems at the beginning, how was I going to cope with an automatic promotion system? I wondered and I did not feel good at all. I knew very well that I was not teaching the children properly in those circumstances. I felt disgusted with myself for standing in front of them supposedly being their teacher, when I knew deep down in my heart that I was not able to.

Out of forty children in my class, if I had to send those without books and school uniforms home, I would be left with ten children. I would have then had a very perfect situation where I would have given proper individual attention, but, at whose expense? I could not live with myself. I could not do it. The easy way out for me was to find a way to leave the system. I was in a state of such turmoil. I was not confused but I had made a decision of teaching outside of South Africa if I could.

Back to our drive to Pietermaritzburg on that Wednesday morning in search of Tata and Thami. As we left Umzimkhulu town after stopping at the Police Charge Office, heading towards Ixopo, I wondered if I was going to see you that day. I did not know where exactly they were going to take me. I was still not allowed to sleep.

I continued counting the road markings. The SB that was not driving kept on asking me about the letters I had written. Why in particular had I written to my father instead of

ESCAPING APARTHEID
A Letter To My Mother

my mother? Was there anybody helping me to write them? Did someone put these ideas in my mind? What did I really feel?

I felt that he did not really think that I was intelligent enough to write the letters to Tata. What I thought was crazy was that while he did not think me intelligent enough to write letters, I was nonetheless intelligent enough to stand in front of a class and teach. That was the craziest set up in Apartheid South Africa. To me that showed how little they cared about black people's education.

On the one hand they had a system they wanted me to be part of, but they did not have confidence in me to be able to write simple letters. Because I was complaining about the injustices of the Apartheid system, it then had to be someone more intelligent than an ordinary black woman teacher to write these letters.

I told him the truth as I felt it. I told him that at school I was faced with children who came from poor families who could not afford all the necessary things that were required. I said the system of South Africa was not fair because his own children went to better schools and had everything taken care of and the government made sure that they were well provided for because they were white. I told him that South Africa was a paradise to him and his family because of the colour of his skin.

I was fed up of their threats and at that point I did not care about going to Robben Island, which they kept on and on about. I must give credit to that man though, he was very patient. He listened to everything that I was saying without showing any nastiness at all. I suppose that is why I found it easy to get my internal frustration out by telling him everything that I felt about the system of South Africa that favoured him as a white man.

But the one that was driving was very defensive at the things that I said. It was strange in a way because I found myself talking to the patient one as though he was someone I knew just because he did not show anger or any touchiness about what I said. Later on I realised that he wanted to win my confidence and wanted me to see him as a friend so I could tell him everything as I was beginning to tell him about the problems that faced blacks and

ESCAPING APARTHEID
A Letter To My Mother

the reasons why I wanted to leave South Africa.

At some point I wanted a break from talking to him so I asked him if I could sleep for a little while. He said he would let me sleep on condition that I categorically promised to point my father out and Thami out, even if they were just walking along the road. He said I had not yet convinced him that I was going to co-operate with them. He said he was not bothered much about my grievances because I would soon get over them and be able to teach the children without worrying about their circumstances.

He said it was natural to feel the way I did because I had just left college not so long ago. He told me that Swaziland was not going to be an answer to my problems because I would find that they had their own problems there that I would still find difficult to cope with anyway. He went on to say that the most important thing for me to do was to make sure that they found Thami and my father because then I would be free to teach without them (SBs) ever troubling me again. That they would not even send the report they were required to send to the Department of Education.

They would tear it up if I assisted them, failing which then I would certainly be sent to Robben Island. Do you know what I decided to do?

We drove past Ixopo—to take mental note of all the scenery around me—which is a town in Natal a lot bigger, at the time, than Umzimkhulu town. I was sure I was not going to point a finger to either Tata or Thami. I was prepared to be sent to their Robben Island. I felt that I might be seeing those areas for the last time. As it turned out, yes I saw them for the last time!

What I remember most was the drive around the Umkhomazi area. I had been around those parts before, but that day it seemed so precious to see the zigzagging bends that seemed to go up and down in a never ending and somewhat frightening manner.

We approached Umkhomazi river from high up and as I looked ahead to my left, I could see the hills dotted with grazing cattle, sheep and goats. Those animals belonged to the people who lived around the area. The vegetation was of mixed wild trees, scattered around and not very tall. Still on my left but further below, I could see the river. It was very wide and its waters were still! I could not help but feel intimidated by its sight. On either side of the road were tree covered cliffs. Losing concentration on that road could be fatal as you well know. But that day it seemed as though I was seeing the area for the first time. Its beauty was mesmerising.

Further to my right at a distance I could see forests and hills. It was a beautiful sight. We drove a few yards on a flat area of the road just as we reached the bottom. But it was not long before the winding bends led us up the hill again. As we climbed up the bends, the view to my right turned to shrubs covering the hill we were climbing. At that point I suppose we would be in Pietermaritzburg not before long.

The scenery then was not very interesting. Towards Pietermaritzburg there were sugar cane farms that were owned by very poor Indians. It is quite possible that they were not really poor but it is just that each time I saw their homes, they screamed of poverty! They were built of corrugated iron sheets for both walls and roofs and were very old and rusty. They just looked pitiful.

Going back to Pietermaritzburg that day under those circumstances brought back painful memories because I was not sure what was to become of me that night. I was convinced that I would spend the night in jail but did not know where.

On arrival at Pietermaritzburg we went to Loop Street Police Station where a very smooth talking, polite black SB man was picked up. He was so different from Vatteman. He was picked, I suppose for his expertise. He was Zulu and very good at his job. He was very persuasive. He told me that he was aware of the fact that I had not had any sleep and that I was not going to have any until I convinced the two white SBs that I would point both Tata and Thami out. He said that to convince the two that this was what I was going to do, I had to convince him first.

As we left Loop Street Police Station, heading for Edendale's slums, where you were living with my young brothers and one of my

ESCAPING APARTHEID
A Letter To My Mother

elder sisters, I could not help but see the poverty and helplessness of the living conditions and the people around Edendale.

One could see the smoke from the shanties, the hopelessness as people moved about their daily chores seemingly having surrendered to poverty, and the problems that came with it. And then there were the sad faces of those who sat aimlessly at doorways—it just seemed so painful with the resignation on people's faces. It also seemed as though their lives had just ended even though they were still breathing!

Now and again the monotonous sight of the shanties was interrupted by either a passenger train or a goods train travelling through Edendale from the Cape Province into the town of Pietermaritzburg. I had travelled in one of these passenger trains now and again from Kokstad during my Teacher Training days.

In that crumbly little shack of a house the SBs went through everything as you know. But do you know what tore me apart? My two little brothers who could not understand what was happening but thought I could give them some money so they could buy sweets. They asked for a cent each and I could not give them anything. That pained me. I did not have two cents and yet I wanted so much to give them something for I knew that I might not see them again since I also felt at the time that I had either to remain in South Africa and go to Robben Island as the SBs persistently threatened, or I had to escape and go to another country. I knew escaping was going to be very difficult and it also seemed impossible. In my mind I desperately wanted to leave South Africa.

I was not going to keep the promise and the SBs were not stupid and sooner than later they would stop threatening but do something about me. My teaching profession was over. I was aware of that, especially when I spoke to the Zulu SB who had been brought from Loop Street. He had said it would take time for the SBs to trust me even if I co-operated. But he said that at least co-operating would allow me to settle down and get married like a good girl should, as I would not be sent to jail on co-operating. He told me to stop getting involved in things that I had no control over.

ESCAPING APARTHEID
A Letter To My Mother

Before swearing and hoping to die should I not point Thami or Tata out to the SBs, I told this gentleman about my observation of how the whites treated Vatteman even though he was a colleague to them. I told him that he, himself, may appear superior while talking to me, in order to help the others who were his colleagues, but on the whole, he was just a "kaffir" not better nor worse than me.

At this he said that what I thought did not matter only he had a job to do and he had a family to support. The manner in which he said this made me smile for he knew what I was saying was true. He smiled too and I promised him that I would help the other SBs on our way back to the Cape Province.

He went and told them that I was going to help. From that time on they smiled and seemed very pleasant and pleased by the fact I was going to certainly help them. I was a sensible girl, they told me. They acted kindly and attentively. They even let me sleep on the way back to the Cape Province. They woke me up at Ixopo and bought me a pint of milk and a packet of assorted biscuits. The one who had been very defensive and arrogant changed his attitude too. They went to a whites-only restaurant. I really enjoyed my treat! A packet of assorted biscuits would have bought a day's meal for our whole family. At some point I felt guilty eating those biscuits because I had not been able to give my brothers a cent each.

They let me sleep all the way to Umzimkhulu. On arrival there I was taken to the Police Charge Office where I was asked to make a statement and in that statement I had to specifically state that I was going to assist them in arresting my father and Thami. I was now believed by the SBs that having signed the statement I was definitely on their side.

They also said that I should be on the lookout for both Tata and Thami as they thought they might still be in the Umzimkhulu district. They said that it was likely that Thami would come back to Gugwini to see me and they gave me a code to use just in case he came during the night. I was to go to the local shop and telephone a certain number in Kokstad and just say, "The Bird Has Arrived" and I did not have to pay the village shop owner for the call because it was going to be paid by them.

I agreed to all of this knowing full well that I was not going to do any of it. I wanted to be given a break because I was very exhausted and sleepy.

12. THE LAST MILES

After all that I had promised we set off, going back the way we had come in during the morning, the Kokstad route. We drove past Clydesdale once more and it was a pleasant sunny afternoon. I was in the SBs good books now. They were convinced that I was definitely going to point out the people they were looking for.

Driving past Clydesdale we went up a winding hill, just before Thembeni. But there is that stretch of road, I mean on the National Road, that does not give much room to pedestrians. In most cases people tend to walk facing oncoming cars. As we drove on this stretch of the road, it was hot and the windows were down and both the SBs were in front.

They had obtained Thami's description from the family he lived with.

I was just about to fall asleep when one of the SBs turned and looked at me saying, "Look, is that not Ngxaliwe (Thami's family name)? Look at that jacket, the balaclava, the features, everything seems to fit the description of him."

I turned my head and looked out. He was behind a group of school children. He saw the car and saw that we were looking at him. I turned to the SB who was waiting for my confirmation. I told him "No, it is not him."

I do not know where I got the confident calm manner but I was convincing. Inside me I was scared! They drove away believing that it was not Thami.

When we turned towards Gugwini I could not believe it. I had thought that I was going to be detained that night. But they drove me to my rented accommodation and I was very pleased. Then I made a terrible mistake. I told the woman who was Thami's distant relative (where he had lived all along) that the SBs had trusted me and had waited for my confirmation of Thami. I did not know that at that time she had already been bought by the

SBs and had been promised a lot of money. Incidentally, I had been promised money too. I had been told that the money I would get would be far more than what I was earning as a teacher.

She reported me to the SBs. That evening Thami came. Since we did not have any other way of communicating other than him coming over for very brief moments to find out what was happening, I became very sensitively intuitive.

Every time he was around I just knew and went outside behind the rondavel I rented, which was where he always stood on the other side of the barbed wire fencing. It was as though we communicated telepathically. These knowing feelings were very intense and forceful.

Thami came to find out why he was not arrested, and what had I told the SBs. I told him everything including what I had told his sister-in law. Telling his sister-law was the biggest mistake he said. He told me that the SBs would come in the morning for me and I had to be prepared for the rough ride.

We both decided that night that we had to escape. We both knew that if I was lucky to be returned to Gugwini when they knew that I had deceived them, it would be because they were using me as a bait to catch him. Since we did not have money we had to wait for my salary which would help us with our escape. That meant waiting for almost a month to the end of June. Thami went away to find people who would help us escape. He already knew that the other members of the organisation had been arrested. He thanked me for my bravery even though that meant I was in more trouble for telling that woman.

He said he had been very scared when he saw the car and saw that we were looking at him. He had known then that they had his description. He said he thought the car was going to turn back any time to pick him up. He had not known whether to run or just continue to walk leisurely. But he continued to walk leisurely. When the car did not return after five minutes he had relaxed a bit and then had found a track that he used which was away from the National Road.

ESCAPING APARTHEID
A Letter To My Mother

The SBs returned the following morning and it was very rough, just like Thami had predicted. I was treated as though I was the most dirtiest, I mean morally, person that ever walked the planet. You should have heard the swearing that was going on.

I was taken to the Police Charge Office at Umzimkhulu for another questioning and yet another statement. They made me stand beneath a light bulb that produced a very hot heat and one of the SBs had a huge stick he frequently lifted as though he was going to beat me and each time I flinched a torrent of insults came my way.

They asked me why I told a lie and why I did not point Thami out. I told them that it was because I loved Thami and I feared they were going to put him away and I would never be able to see him again.

They asked me if I was still a virgin and if I slept with Thami and what did Thami see in me or what did I see in him. They told me that I was not worth a single look from any man and that I had a flat bum that was not attractive. They said a lot of things that were so humiliating and debasing, things that I cannot write.

I was at some point taken out of the interview room and asked to stand a few yards from the water tap that was used by men in cells, for washing their plates. They let men who had been members of the same organisation as Thami and lived in the neighbouring villages not far from Gudlintaba, come out of their cells to wash their plates from the water tap. It was obvious that these men had been severely tortured because they were finding it difficult to walk. They winced each time they put their bare feet down on the ground and walked very slowly.

When all the men had come out and gone back to their cells, they took me inside under the hot light bulb again. They asked if I knew the last man who had come out. This man had bruises on his face as well as on his hands and arms and was wearing a pair of trousers and a vest. It was Thami's real brother-in-law who was married to one of his twin sisters.

I told them that I had never seen the man before. I felt then that it was not going to be long before they took me in. I was also glad that Thami and I had already decided to run away from South Africa. It was a very frightening time though. I never asked Thami where he stayed and I did not want to know.

After another statement at the Police Charge Office, I was driven back to Gugwini. My landlady and everyone around me had been asked not to talk to me. I felt very isolated. But there was one special teacher (who I thought was a lot older than you), Miss Nodola, who completely understood what was going on and she never stopped talking to me. I appreciated her and still do.

Both of us were in the thatched buildings a distance away from the main school. Many times when the SBs came swearing and shouting at me to come out of the classroom, children petrified, she would take my pupils to her classroom and teach them all. In her I was able to confide and she was very understanding. She was like a mother to me in the end.

One evening before we escaped, while still waiting for the month end salary, Tata paid me a surprise visit. He had been arrested and released but I do not know where and how. I did not ask him.

I also do not know what they had done to his finger. He was in pain. His middle finger was bandaged and it was a strain for him to lift his arm. I knew he had been tortured. When I asked him what had happened to his finger, he only said, "Oh, it's nothing really." Tata did not stay long. He had come to plead with me not to leave South Africa so I could help you because he could not get a job and his situation was even worse now, tangled with the SBs.

He was in pain to explain how he could not get a proper job. Long before he had burnt his 'dom pass', he had been a police officer but had lost his job because he had arrested a white man he had caught stealing. Instead of calling his white superiors to deal with the incident, he had taken it upon himself to arrest the man and taken him to the Police Charge Office. A black police man had no right arresting a white man, he had been told by his superiors. So he was sacked and could never get a job as a police man again in South Africa after that incident.

ESCAPING APARTHEID
A Letter To My Mother

I told Tata that even if I did not escape, there was no future for me in South Africa, as I was always going to be watched and not trusted by the Police Special Branch. I told him that they had been threatening me with Robben Island and I believed they would take me there as soon as they were unable to find Thami. When Tata realised that we had no option but to leave the country, he just said, "Please look after yourself." We hugged and he left. That was the last time I ever saw him.

When he died in 1981 I remembered Gugwini and his bandaged finger and I wept full of bitterness towards the South African Apartheid system.

Back at Majola's and Khwezi's hide out, that evening, we decided that Khwezi was going to pretend to be me, and go cash my pay cheque. It was a risky situation but we reckoned that since it was going to be a Saturday and very busy with all teachers from the Umzimkhulu district, the cashiers would not have time to look at people's faces as long as they submitted a signed cheque, which I had signed.

We also thought that the Police Special Branch officers would not think that we had been waiting for my salary and had to cash it at Umzimkhulu town. As it turned out Khwezi just joined the long queue of teachers waiting to cash their pay cheques, kept quiet, and never spoke to anyone. When her turn came, she presented the cheque with my signature and was handed the money by the cashier. It was that easy and such a relief! Do you know what was later funny to me? Finding out that Thami was hiding not far from the Police Station at Umzimkhulu during all that time. One of his school friends worked as a prison officer and let him stay with him.

With the money we were able to hire a man Majola trusted who did not even know that he was carrying people being sought by the Police Special Branch. He drove us to Harding where we took taxis to Durban. It was a Monday morning.

Four days had gone by since we left Gugwini village. We worked out that if we stayed until the Monday, the SBs would have been very busy on the Friday morning when they realised that I was not around. They had been turning up every day at school to check on me and to find out whether Thami had contacted me.

It was very scary in the van because we had to behave as normal travellers but at the same time avoid being recognised. I wore a black and white dog tooth tight fitting check skirt and white blouse. I put on a nice black hat that made me look very sophisticated. Even the SBs would not have recognised me. But I was shaking with fear in my whole being.

The van drove towards Gugwini and when we were approaching Mr White's home (the taxi man), I nearly messed myself because I was thinking that the SBs perhaps had stationed themselves at his house to see who was driving past as there were very few motor vehicles around Gugwini.

At Harding, we had to get off at a junction for taxis to Durban. The van driver knew where to drop us. As we stood there waiting for taxis, I was sweating with fear in case the SBs were looking for us that Monday morning.

Fortunately we did not wait long because a taxi pulled up that had a space for two people. At that point I knew that our ancestors were with us all the way. It was going to be easier in Durban as the Special Branch would not know where to start looking for us. Majola and Thami had assured me of this.

In Durban we travelled to Mlazi Township where another of Thami's friend knew people we could live with. We stayed with people who were trusted and knew that we were running away from the SBs and so we had to stay indoors all the time, and they also made sure that the neighbours did not know they were hiding people.

I used to stand by the window and just watch people who could not see me from behind the net curtains, walking up and down the streets, chatting and going about their business. One day when I was standing by the window, my heart jumped with excitement for a second but soon went into depression because I had seen my cousin, Nonzwakazi.

She was so beautiful, walking down the road wearing a pink floral dress. I wanted to speak to her and leave a message for you. But I could not because I was hiding. I was running away from the Special Branch.

ESCAPING APARTHEID
A Letter To My Mother

I called Thami to come see her. I cried and actually realised then that my life had completely changed and I did not even know how long I was going to be in that hiding place. There were financial difficulties. Thami's friends had to raise money for our tickets out of Durban to Swaziland. It was a hard call for all of them because they did not earn much money but they had amazing spirits for they were still willing to help us out of South Africa.

It meant we had to stay in Durban until sufficient money was found for us. As it turned out we were in Durban for three months, that is July, August, September. It was very difficult. There were times we were not even sure that these people would really be able to raise enough money for us to leave South Africa.

Food also was very scarce. There were days we did not have anything to eat. The people who were helping us did not have enough money themselves and we understood. The hardest thing was to sit there doing absolutely nothing and read the same book over and over again because there were no books. All our books had been taken by the SBs.

We did not have money to buy anything. It was difficult to cough when the owners of the house we hid in were out during the day because we had to make sure that their neighbours did not get suspicious. We used to take a pillow and put around our mouths when we needed to cough. The most important thing that God helped us with was we never sneezed while in those hiding places. How lucky is that!

We were being looked after by invisible beings, I am sure of this. From the first safe place we lived at, we moved to another part of Mlazi Township where we stayed for two months. It was hard for most people because some of the people who were originally going to help finance our escape, had also depended on others to help out but had been let down. But eventually enough money was raised for us to travel to Hluhluwe where we would make our way by foot to Swaziland.

From Durban we took a train to Mtubatuba and from there a bus to Hluhluwe. Our plan was to travel by foot to Golela, a town in Swaziland bordering South Africa. Just before we got out of the bus at Hluhluwe which was the last stop for everybody, we saw a lot of

Special Branch officers at the parking area.

The good thing about the Special Branch officers is that they were easy to pick out because they were always very conspicuous in an area where only black people lived and they always looked very well fed and their cars were most of the time Ford makes.

There was an old lady who was sitting close to us. Thami just turned to the old lady and said quietly, "Ma, we are at your mercy now. We are running away from them out there. Please help us. We do not know this area."

The old lady smiled at both of us and said, "Do not worry. You are my grandchildren visiting me should anyone ask. Do not worry that you speak Xhosa; I can have Xhosa speaking grand children. There is no law against that. I am Mrs Zondi. So you are Zondis and please leave all the talking to me and just walk leisurely with me and carry my bags here (handing her bag to Thami). You, young girl, come hold my hand and help me out. Walk with me slowly but purposefully."

We thanked the old lady.

We got out of the bus, walking leisurely and purposefully as Mrs Zondi had instructed. She whispered, *Do not look back. Keep walking and mingle with the crowds.* We followed her instructions. We walked out of the station, and when we were about two hundred yards away from the station, she turned and looked back and then with a smile on her face said, "You can both relax now. God has been with us and your ancestors are all with you. Now come to my house and stay there until it is dark. We will give you directions of how to get out of this location."

We thanked her and went with her to her house. We offered her money for food but she refused it saying, "Please keep whatever money you have, I have enough food for all of us tonight. God will provide for tomorrow. You have a long journey ahead of you and you are going to need every cent you have."

We were so grateful to this old lady, it just seemed like she was an angel sent to guide us on our last miles before we completely left South Africa. The truth was that we really did not have enough money. So we were grateful

ESCAPING APARTHEID
A Letter To My Mother

for any few cents that we could hold on to for the journey ahead.

When it was dark, Mrs Zondi asked her two grand children (a boy and a girl), who were about fifteen years old, to accompany us as far as the edge of the location where we would continue walking until we came to a barbed wire fencing which was the start of the Hluhluwe game reserve.

She bid us farewell and wished us all the best. But because it was too dark, we thanked the kids and asked them to go back to be with their grand mother as we were fine on our own. It was one of those nights when the moon came out late so it was very dark.

In no time, though, our eyes were used to the darkness as we walked to the end of the location and we continued walking for about twenty more minutes before we came to a high barbed wire fencing. On the other side of the fencing the vegetation was of thorny bushes which are usually called 'vag 'n bitjie' (wait a bit). This is because the thorns just keep stopping you as they are either holding on to your clothes or you are trying to avoid them scratching your eyes out.

NOMANONO ISAACS

We crawled underneath the barbed wire and were at the mercy of the vag 'n bitjie thorns. The bushes were dense and we had to be very quiet because we did not want to be caught by the patrol guards. My heart was pounding so hard and loudly with fear I thought Thami could hear it because I asked him if he could hear it. He said he could not hear mine but could hear his too.

At this I could not stop laughing but it was a weird laugh because it was a mixture of something funny to laugh at as well as very frightening. I also had to laugh quietly and it was very difficult. Amongst the dense bushes, as we proceeded slowly trying not to make noise with our foot steps, now and again we would stop dead on our tracks, seeing what we thought was a person ahead of us, waiting to pounce on us. These were images of the bushes in front of us with light from the sky showing in the background. It was very scary!

The frustration of constantly having to untangle ourselves from the thorny bushes made us decide that it would be best to only walk a distance of about two miles into the game reserve, even though under those circumstances and the darkness, we could not realistically work out the distance.

We walked as far as we could into the heart of the game reserve and then found a clearing and slept there after praying that no snakes and dangerous animals come our way. During the night there was an animal that did not seem too far from us which constantly howled and we did not even know what it was until later when we talked to someone and we described the sound. We were told that the sound we described was that of a hyena's. God's angels were with us. Just before dawn we got up and started again. This time we could see the foot tracks clearly and just followed them as long as they were going North East. We walked fast in order to be out of South Africa as soon as we could.

When the sun came out it was very hot. By ten in the morning it felt as though it was midday.

We walked for about two hours within the game reserve before we saw people's homes. Because there was no tangible border mark between South Africa and Swaziland, we decided that we would ask for water in the homes that we passed, and from speaking to the people, we would then be able to tell from the language they spoke whether we were in South Africa or not. That is what we did and in some cases, just asked people directly if they were in Swaziland or South Africa.

It was after midday when we were told that we were in Swaziland. We were exhausted, hungry, dusty and sweaty with yet some more blisters on my feet, but we were jubilant! I wanted to jump for joy but did not have strength in my body. So I just sat on the grass and wept with relief but at the same time knowing that Golela was still miles away and there was still more walking to be done on my blistered feet.

I wept for my family back in South Africa especially for you, for I knew I was not going to be able to help you.

I thought of the suffering that was going to be turned on you, for I had left the country. It was well known that the family of those who had run away from South African politics, were always the victims of the SBs. But I was relieved that I was not going to be threatened with Robben Island again. I felt relieved and positive that I had a new beginning ahead of me. I will let you know later how my life was in Swaziland, Botswana, Uganda, and now here in the UK. Until then, take care. I love you.

EPILOGUE

Once safely in Swaziland, Nomanono married Thami. After being there a while she woke up one day with an overwhelming thought that she should write to the South African Police, asking them not to torture or punish her mother or any of her relations. They did not know that she was going to leave nor did they know that she was against the South African system.

It was well known that families of those who had fled had been tortured by the South African Special Branch Police, and so she wrote, addressing the letter to The Chief Superintendent, South African Police, Loop Street, Pietermaritzburg, Republic of South Africa. She did not know the correct address but reckoned that they would get it.

As it turned out, when she was finally able to visit South Africa after twenty-six years in exile, her Mother praised her for setting her free. Her words were: "Thank you my beautiful brave daughter for setting me FREE! The letter you sent to Pietermaritzburg Police Station, set me FREE! (And her mother, did a little happy dance as she uttered these words, filled with joy!)

"For six months after you left, all my neighbours were told not to talk to me. I was not to talk to anyone. Every morning, the Special Branch Police came to pick me up and drove me to my place of work. When I finished work, in the afternoon or evening, they collected me to take me home.

"So this one morning, one of the police came smiling and waving a piece of paper saying, 'Mama, you are Free! Here is a letter from your daughter setting you Free! I have been told by my Superiors, to come and tell you that we are not going to trouble you ever again!'"

Nomanono was told by her mother that she had also not been allowed to bring home anything that belonged to Nomanono from the family where she rented accommodation. That family had been given strict instructions by the

ESCAPING APARTHEID
A Letter To My Mother

Special Branch not to give Nomanono's mother or any of her relatives the bed and cooking pots, which were the only things Nomanono possessed.

It is then that Nomanono completely understood why, when she was able to write to her mother from the United Kingdom, her mother always said to her 'please do not visit me, however much you miss me.'

The pain in Nomanono's heart stopped instantly after on her first visit to South Africa in 26 years since leaving, and that is when she realised that what she thought was a heart problem (and had talked to doctors about a constant painfully throbbing heart beat), was truly because she 'missed' her mother. She continued to visit her mother, enjoying supporting her together with her other siblings until she transitioned in 2007 at the ripe old age of 83.

The Special Branch had eventually believed that Tata had nothing to do with Nomanono's dislike of the South African system. He was passionate about becoming a herbalist when Nomanono last spoke with him on his one and only fateful visit. And when

Nomanono visited South Africa, she was able to see her late father's certificates. He had qualified as a Herbalist but unfortunately he had died of a heart attack at the age of 58.

Since Nomanono had qualified as a primary school teacher, she did fulfil her desires to be a teacher in Swaziland. And she enjoyed teaching arithmetic and music. Music was something that she believed was in her soul and she revelled in teaching pupils how to sing. According to Nomanono, even those children who thought they did not have good voices were transformed into beautiful songbirds under her tutelage and her love of music. She taught school at Hlathikhulu District.

There were always music competitions in Southern Africa, something enjoyed by a lot of teachers as well as pupils, but in the particular school where Nomanono taught, when the music competition times were announced and discussed by all the teachers, she volunteered to conduct a senior choir. There were enough children in that school to have three choirs entering the district music competitions: senior, intermediate, and junior choirs.

ESCAPING APARTHEID
A Letter To My Mother

Seeing how enthusiastic Nomanono was with music, other teachers asked if she could teach them how to conduct their choirs and more importantly, to teach them to teach the children to sing. This was not a problem for Nomanono. She did this with her big heart, amazing love and enthusiasm. To cut a long story short, that school ended up with three trophies at a District Level of competition: For the Junior Choir, Intermediate Choir and Senior Choir.

Nomanono's Senior Choir had to represent the whole district of Hlathikhulu at Manzini (one of Swaziland's towns) where various districts were competing. Nomanono was the youngest conductor of a senior choir, competing with people the same age as her father (who had been in the business for years).

This did not trouble Nomanono in any way, saying that she felt invincible where conducting and teaching children to sing was concerned. She was driven to perfecting her pupils' performances. The choir earned second place and her school took a trophy back to Hlathikhulu District. The applause and joy from all the teachers from her district was just phenomenal and to her it was as if her school had come in first.

During this time in her life, not only was Nomanono happy with her music, she had an infant daughter.

From Swaziland Thami and Nomanono went to Botswana where their second daughter was born. From Botswana they moved to Uganda where Nomanono got a job as a primary school teacher and renewed her enthusiasm for music as there were other teachers there who enjoyed singing like she did. However, Thami's and Nomanono's marriage had difficulties and it eventually ended.

Thami obtained a BA degree from the University of Makerere in Uganda and later obtained a PhD in Philosophy from the University of Khartoum. He later joined the ANC and is now happily remarried and retired in South Africa, after many years of teaching.

While still in Uganda, Nomanono decided that she no longer wanted to teach and moved to Kenya to train at Reeswood Secretarial

College to become a secretary. When she returned to Kampala, in Uganda, she worked as a secretary. When she later got political asylum in the United Kingdom and later became a British citizen, she enjoyed bringing up her two wonderful daughters which became her life's purpose.

Later, when her daughters became adults, in a funny, wonderful way they became her great inspiration for life and to live life to the fullest possibility! She now enjoys her grandchildren, secure in the fact that they will never have to escape apartheid.

ABOUT THE AUTHOR

NOMANONO ISAACS was born in the small, remote village of Makhanya, in the District of Umzimkhulu, in South Africa where she enjoyed a childhood filled with music, laughter and love—not just from her extended family but also from her community.

All that changed at the age of 12 when the South African Apartheid government embarked on Rehabilitation Schemes in Black residential areas, which meant a lot of hardship for most people. Her whole world view fell apart.

At the age of 20 she escaped to the neighbouring nation of Swaziland, eventually making her way to England, where she now lives.

Printed on 100% Recycled Paper
ACID FREE — ARCHIVAL GRADE